USING LITERATURE TO SUPPORT SKILLS AND CRITICAL DISCUSSION FOR STRUGGLING READERS

Grades 3–9

Nancy S. Williams

ScarecrowEducation
Lanham, Maryland • Toronto • Oxford
2004

Published in the United States of America
by ScarecrowEducation
An imprint of The Rowman & Littlefield Publishing Group, Inc.
4501 Forbes Boulevard, Suite 200, Lanham, Maryland 20706
www.scarecroweducation.com

PO Box 317
Oxford
OX2 9RU, UK

British Library Cataloguing in Publication Information Available

Library of Congress Cataloging-in-Publication Data

Williams, Nancy S.
   Using literature to support skills and critical discussion
for struggling readers : grades 3–9 / Nancy S. Williams.
      p. cm.
   Includes bibliographical references (p.   ) and index.
   ISBN 1-57886-096-2 (pbk. : alk. paper)
   1. Reading—Remedial teaching. 2. Children—Books and reading. I. Title.
LB1050.5 .W48945 2004
372.43—dc22

                                        2003023552

To Randy, for his support
and to Eve, for her inspiration

CONTENTS

FIGURES

ACKNOWLEDGMENTS

Many colleagues and friends have contributed to this project. I would like to thank my DePaul colleagues: Penny Silvers, for her careful reading and insightful comments, and Marie Donovan, Kate Liston, and Sonia Soltero, who have generously shared resources that have supported this project. I would be at a loss without the enthusiasm and encouragement from Mary and Ernie Cherullo, lifetime public school educators. I am grateful to David Powers for his creative technology skills and to Lynn Stuertz, who always greets me with suggestions and a handful of books when I visit the Book Stall, Winnetka. A special thanks to Randy Williams, for his diligent reading of my text, good critique, and constant support. Finally, this book would not have been possible without the talents and remarkable capabilities of both the graduate students and school-age children with whom I have had the privilege to work.

INTRODUCTION

All students need reading experiences that engage them, good stories with characters who grow and develop, and characters that they care about, can identify with, and from whom they can learn. This applies as much to struggling readers as to those students who read without difficulty. Literacy skills are deepened when readers enthusiastically talk about stories, make inferences about characters' actions, and predict outcomes based on what they know and have read. Quality literature has authentic situations that invite discussion and analysis. From Jon Scieszka's humorous short chapter-book series about the *Time Warp Trio* to Kate DiCamillo's heartwarming *Because of Winn-Dixie* (a Newbery Honor book) and Walter Dean Myers's compelling *Monster* (Prinz Award for young adult fiction), wonderful literature abounds for struggling readers to learn from, make personal connections to, and enjoy. Having worked several decades with students with reading difficulties, I have observed the enthusiasm and engagement of children and adolescents when captivated with a good book that is on their reading level. One twelve-year-old struggling reader said that she didn't know stories could sound so real until she started reading Betsy Byars's mystery *Death's Door* about the suspenseful episodes of Herculeah Jones. Thus began her love affair with Betsy Byars's red-headed sleuth.

Discouraged readers will become motivated readers only when they find readable books that interest them. Students with reading difficulties have strengths and talents to celebrate, and enjoy books that relate to background experiences and interests. For example, a gifted ballet student was excited to read fiction and nonfiction trade books about dancing, a child fascinated with magic was mesmerized by a nonfiction book on how to perform magic tricks (a good opportunity to read and practice sequencing skills), and a sensitive teenager fond of animals eagerly read Avi's moving fantasy *The Good Dog* (2001) and Gary Paulson's nonfiction autobiography, *My Life in Dog Years* (1998). All three students were receiving support for academic problems that included decoding, reading comprehension, and spelling. Chandler-Olcott encourages teachers to learn more about student preferences in order to recommend books and allow students to make choices on their own. "When teachers encourage students to make choices on their own, they create a space in classroom communities for individual's passions and interests" (2002, 18). After years of observing and studying exemplary classroom practices, Allington notes that effective teachers provide a variety of books that children *can* read and choices about books they *will* read (2002, 746).

Further, students want to read about characters that are like them, characters that overcome obstacles to solve problems and reach goals. Stringer and Mollineaux note that underachieving reluctant readers may underestimate what they are capable of becoming and when reading becomes more meaningful it connects to their search for something worthwhile (2003, 75). Rich characters jump from pages speaking different languages and experiencing different customs and cultures yet they struggle with universal problems such as peer relations, school failures, and conflicting family relationships. One sensitive ten-year-old struggling reader who was reading *Holes* (Sachar) said that he knew why Zero had run away when Mr. Sir called him stupid. He quietly added that he would have done the same thing. Well-developed characters like Zero and Stanley Yelnats in Sachar's fascinating fantasy bring life to reading and meaning to readers.

I have selected children's literature as a springboard from which to develop critical discussion and higher-level thinking skills. I use critical discussion in this book to refer to discussions that provide students with opportunities to make personal connections with the story; to evaluate and reflect upon these experiences; and to examine character perspectives, attitudes, and social issues that arise in specific literature selections. I focus on biography, fiction, and verse as genres that inspire, motivate, and create opportunities for self-reflection and literacy development. I include over one hundred selections of good books with reading levels accessible to struggling readers (i.e., reading levels below interest levels) to provide teachers with choices that appeal to a variety of interests for students who demonstrate reading difficulty. I highlight specific selections that represent the rich diversity that is evident in today's classrooms (See chapter 1, "How to Make Connections between Reader and Text"). Morocco and Hindin write about the good discussions that readers with reading and writing disabilities have when talking about Sharon Flake's character Maleeka in *The Skin I'm In*. According to these authors, "Good adolescent literature is filled with authentic dilemmas such as Maleeka's that capture the minds of middle school students and stimulate their motivation to read" (2002, 144). A middle school reader wrote the following review about *The Skin I'm In*: "I want to thank my teacher, Miss Jenkins, for reading that book to the class, and that's why I reread it over the summer. I think people who are having trouble with the skin they are in should read it" (The Book Report 2003, 5). Maleeka is one of many such characters that students will discover in chapter 3," Book Descriptions, Discussions, and Extensions. "I do not include high-interest, low-readability books that contain controlled vocabulary and a simplified sentence structure. Rather, this book includes children's literature selections written by respected authors that are rich in story, character development, and language, inviting struggling readers to enter intriguing worlds of realism and mystery and meet characters much like themselves.

The book contains four chapters. Chapter 1, "How to Make Connections between Reader and Text," addresses the importance of matching books to students' reading levels, interests, and background experiences, and includes examples of quality children's literature that motivate struggling readers. It is important that students see themselves in the characters they read. Students with reading difficulties, like all readers, represent a diverse group that includes cultural, racial, language, ability, and physiological differences. Chapter 1 highlights books with rich characters that represent the diversity in today's classrooms, and protagonists who use strengths to overcome difficulties and reach goals—an important message for struggling readers who often lack self-confidence in their abilities to succeed.

Chapter 2, "How to Develop Literacy Skills and Higher-Level Thinking," examines how children's literature supports critical discussion and provides opportunities for struggling readers to talk about what they know, what they have read, and what they think. Literature selections (e.g., poetry, fairy tales, easy text for older readers) highlight descriptive vocabulary, figurative language (similes, metaphors, idioms), and complex characters and multilayered themes that support critical discussion and higher-level thinking skills. Chapter 2 also addresses the importance of student reflection, describes the role of graphic organizers in facilitating discussion, and describes literature opportunities for mathematical extensions and problem solving.

Chapter 3, "Book Descriptions, Discussions, and Extensions," contains over one hundred quality children's literature selections appropriate for struggling readers (i.e., with estimated reading levels below interest levels). Selections are categorized by interest and genre (e.g., nonfiction—sports, fine arts, writers, leaders of social justice; fantasy—animals, ghosts, fairy tales, mystery) and include literature descriptions (synopsis, estimated reading levels, interest levels, number of pages) and five to eight discussion questions and extensions that promote literacy skills and higher-level thinking. Questions are used as a springboard to engage students in self-reflection and in-depth literature discussions. For example, students make connections with the text, infer and predict, discuss and use descriptive vocabulary and figurative language, evaluate story, and examine character perspectives, attitudes, and theme-based cultural and social issues. Extensions promote inquiry through web research, as well as writing, art, and drama activities that support and extend reading comprehension. Discussion questions and extensions are appropriate for individual tutorial or remediation settings, special education classrooms, general education and inclusion classrooms, and help teachers facilitate literature discussions in a variety of formats that include literature discussion groups, self-regulated reading (the Four-Blocks Literacy Model, by Cunningham), book club discussions and response writing, guided reading, and whole class discussions.

Chapter 4, "Resources," includes professional literature and technology resources such as websites for children's literature, interactive literacy activities and games, sites directed to special needs, author websites, children's books available on audiotape, as well as resources for parents and caregivers.

Three appendixes follow chapter 4: appendix A and appendix B include a listing of children's book titles by interest and genre, respectively; appendix C provides examples of idioms and familiar expressions in specific literature selections described in chapter 3.

Discussion is essential to literacy development. According to Ada and Campoy, dialogue invites students to share personal experiences, make connections with text, and engage in higher-order thinking skills (2004, 41). Standards for the English language arts (sponsored by the National Council of Teachers of English and the International Reading Association) state that students apply knowledge of language structures, language conventions, figurative language, and genre to create, critique, and discuss text. Critical discussion and higher-level thinking are elements included in the 2000 National Reading Panel Report as critical to creating successful readers (Mandel Morrow 2003). A goal of this book is to provide struggling readers with good books that they can read and that make connections with their lives, and opportunities to discuss these books in ways that support self-reflection and higher-level thinking.

A colleague, friend, and veteran of thirty years of teaching children with reading difficulties noted that often her poor readers were viewed as poor thinkers and that this could not be further from the truth. Her students were eager for opportunities to read stories about authentic characters and situations and were good at questions that connected to their lives. Further, her students used idioms, metaphors, and similes in their daily language (e.g., "Tyler looks like a clown"; "Erica is hanging loose"). She just needed to expand their thinking and usage to include more descriptive (and in some cases, more appropriate) vocabulary like the rich examples found in quality children's literature. Figurative language creates potent images, and imaging is a powerful tool in strengthening reading comprehension. What better way than to read, model, and discuss the rich language contained in children's literature. As my colleague noted, "Kids can get that unless we believe they can't!"

REFERENCES

Ada, A. F., and F. I. Campoy. 2004. *Authors in the classroom: A transformative educational process*. New York: Pearson Education.

Allington, R. 2002. What I've learned about effective reading instruction from a decade of studying exemplary elementary classroom teachers. *Phi Delta Kappan* 83, no. 10:740–47.

The Book Report. 2003. *The Chicago Tribune*, "Books," August 10, 2003, 5.

Chandler-Olcott, K. 2002. Scaffolding love: A framework for choosing books for, with, and by adolescents. *Illinois Reading Council Journal* 30, no. 2:10–23.

Cunningham, P. 2001. *The four-blocks literacy model: How and why it really works with Patricia Cunningham*. Greensboro, N.C.: Carson-Dellosa.

Mandel Morrow, L. 2003. *Reading Today* 20, no. 6:6.

Morocco, C., and A. Hindin. 2002. The role of conversation in a thematic understanding of literature. *Learning Disabilities Research and Practice* 17, no. 3:144–59.

Stringer, S., and B. Mollineaux. 2003. Removing the word "reluctant" from "reluctant reader." *English Journal* 92, no. 4:71–76.

①

HOW TO MAKE CONNECTIONS
BETWEEN READER AND TEXT

Struggling readers do not usually spend time reading. Reading is difficult and, they say, boring. On their own, they seldom take time or know how to find books that make connections with their lives, ones they can successfully read, and ones that are rich in believable characters and story. According to McCormick (2003), delayed readers have often learned to dislike and avoid books. She notes, however, that "at all grade levels, use of charming, funny, fascinating, exciting, compelling literature encourages students to seek out books as friends, rather than regard them as enemies from which to escape" (191). Standards for reading professionals require teachers to use student interest and backgrounds as a foundation for enjoyment in the reading and writing processes, to select appropriate materials that represent multiple levels and backgrounds, and to use materials that motivate all students to read (see International Reading Association, www.reading.org).

A good teacher is able to match books to the needs and interests of the reader. Books must not only address interest but they must be on the appropriate reading level (RL)—*independent* for reading without assistance and *instructional* for reading with some support. Students understand 90 percent of the text and recognize 98 percent of words at the independent level and understand 70 percent or more of the text and recognize 90 to 97 percent of words at the instructional level (Leslie and Caldwell 2001). If students are truly engaged in reading and can't put the book down, then the book is not too difficult (Calkin et al. 1998). Resources, such as Fountas and Pinnell's *Matching Books to Readers* (1999) and Gunning's *Best Books for Beginning Readers* (1998), provide lists of recommended books according to designated reading levels for beginning readers (K–3). Further, all readers need to see themselves in the literature, not as secondary characters or "other" but as the main character (Harste 2003, 8). The following sections address student interest and highlight books that celebrate diversity through rich, authentic characters and conflicts that explore differences, multiple perspectives, and our universal human characteristics.

STUDENT INTEREST

Student tastes vary. Some students like fantasy—there is always a hero sent on a quest to make an impact on the world (Thomas 2003, 60). A twelve-year-old student receiving reading support was so enthralled with Jerry Spinelli's *Stargirl* (2002)—a riveting, believable fantasy that explores themes of jealously, discrimination, and peer pressure—that she skipped breaks to continue reading about the extraordinary female character that changed lives by refusing to be someone other than herself. A fourteen-year-old giggled, his shoulders softly shaking, as he took turns reading *Bunnicula: A Rabbit Tale of Mystery* (Howe and Howe 1979) with his tutor. The humorous fantasy provided numerous opportunities to recognize, discuss, and enjoy humor, often an evasive skill for struggling readers.

Reluctant readers want plots with action, realistic language, well-defined characters, characters who are their age or slightly older who face tough choices and conflicts, and true-life stories of sport figures, celebrities, musicians, and politicians (Beers 2002, 286–90). Worthy notes that intermediate-grade readers have varied tastes and choose trade books that are mysteries, books with scary themes, humorous stories, books about sports, series books, and books with relevant characters and themes (2002, 568). When reading Betsy Byars's exciting and descriptive *Dead Letter: A Herculeah Jones Mystery* (1996), an engrossed eleven-year-old told her reading tutor that she liked the book because the writing helped her see pictures in her head. Indeed, Byars's use of figurative language and imagery swept the reader into Herculeah's world of mystery and suspense. Another middle school struggling reader, intrigued with Myers's sympathetic character Steve Harmon in *Monster* (1999), provided insightful comments and questions while discussing this riveting contemporary, realistic novel about a sixteen-year-old accused of a felony murder.

Picture books increase motivation, conceptual understanding, aesthetic appreciation, and provide easier, shorter material for older, struggling readers (Carr et al. 2001, 146). Some struggling readers have strong artistic skills; choosing books with quality illustrations stimulates their interest (McCormick 2003, 191). Picture books with mature themes provide successful reading experiences and motivate students with word identification problems. A middle school student with poor decoding skills was immediately caught up in the rich illustrations and fascinating text of the striking picture book *Champion: The Story of Muhammad Ali* (Haskins 2002). The student's interest in Ali, his background knowledge about the famous African American, and the realistic paintings by Eric Velasquez supported reading decoding and subsequent discussions about the extraordinary boxer. Intrigued and motivated by the bold paintings, the young man copied several of Ali's poems and illustrated them. After reading Eve Bunting's historical fiction picture book *The Train to Somewhere* (1996) about orphans traveling west for adoption, a twelve-year-old struggling reader researched the web to discover more about the orphan trains that transported children from New York orphanages to the West, often to futures that were more bleak than those they left behind. She then used a Venn diagram to compare her research to characters and events in Bunting's book. Again, a picture book was successful in captivating a reader's interest and paving the way for literacy development.

Struggling readers make connections with individuals who have similar interests and experience problems and challenges. Biographies are important avenues to reading for many students with reading difficulties. For example, in *Bad Boy: A Memoir* (Myers 2001), Walter Dean Myers describes growing up in Harlem, being part of a loving and structured family, his speech problems, school difficulties (he often was reprimanded for conduct problems), and his love of reading and writing that provided solace and an avenue for success. In *My Life in Dog Years*, Gary Paulsen (1998) describes his bumpy road to success and the memorable dogs that literally saved and gave meaning to his life. After reading *My Life in Dog Years*, a bright teenager and dog lover receiving reading support began Paulsen's adventure stories about Brian Robeson (*Hatchet* 1987; *Brian's Winter* 1996). A boy who was only interested in nonfiction, especially dogs, became fascinated by the excitement of realistic fiction. A seventh-grade English teacher writes about the impact of a biography video about author Gary Paulsen that described his academic problems and his discovery of reading (with the help of a caring librarian) that helped to turn a life of failure into one of success and productivity. After seeing the film, students with similar academic challenges signed out more of Paulsen's books to read (Stringer and Mollineaux 2003, 7). A fifth-grade sports enthusiast receiving reading support made personal connections with David Adler's easy-to-read, moving biography of baseball legend Lou Gehrig, *Lou Gehrig: The Luckiest Man* (1997). He delighted in showing his tutor his knowledge of baseball heroes when he completed an Anticipation Guide, a format that activates students' knowledge about a topic before reading and provides a purpose for subsequent reading (Tierney and Readence 2000, 325). (See figure 1.1) He and his tutor read the statements before reading, discussing and checking off on a teacher-prepared worksheet whether the statements were true or false. After checking "yes" (true) or "no" (false), they continued

Anticipation Guide
Text: *Lou Gehrig: The Luckiest Man* (Adler 1997)

Before Reading		Statements	After Reading	
Yes	No		Yes	No
____	____	1. Lou Gehrig was a baseball player.	____	____
____	____	2. Lou loved all sports.	____	____
____	____	3. Lou's mother encouraged his love of baseball.	____	____
____	____	4. Lou first played for the Kansas City Royals.	____	____
____	____	5. Lou never missed a day of school.	____	____
____	____	6. Lou never missed a game.	____	____
____	____	7. Because of Lou's health he was asked to leave the team.	____	____
____	____	8. Lou worked for the New York City Parole Commission.	____	____
____	____	9. Lou died of a heart attack.	____	____
____	____	10. The week of Lou's death the Yankee game was canceled.	____	____

Figure 1.1. Lou Gehrig Anticipation Guide

taking turns reading, with the "ah ha!" echoed by both as they confirmed or found out new information that would change their prior predictions.

Further, struggling readers feel more like authentic readers when they have a "real" book in their hands. Various strengths, background experiences, and interests trigger a fascination with fiction and nonfiction trade books, ranging from topics about magicians, baseball players, and animals (especially dogs and cats), to characters involved in real-life problems and challenges. Most students request books that pertain to interests and background experiences. Some shrug their shoulders and need more probing to discover a book that might uncover a hidden interest or talent. However, once students encounter a successful reading experience, they are more apt to select other books (often by the same author) and genres that they have not previously read or enjoyed. Struggling readers, most of whom have decoding difficulties, reflect rich experiences and demonstrate higher-level thinking skills when they are given opportunities to respond to and ask questions about good literature in which they have a genuine interest.

STUDENT BACKGROUND: DIVERSITY AND MULTIPLE PERSPECTIVES

An important factor pertaining to student interest is discovering characters with whom individual readers can relate. Books that are rich in diversity and multiple perspectives make connections to readers who find that there are characters like themselves. Worthy and Sailors (2001) describe how a recent immigrant from Mexico turned up her nose at the series books her peers were reading but when she discovered books written by Mexican authors, stories with Spanish words embedded in the text, she proudly pronounced the words with a flair (569). A Latina student remarked that *Esperanza Rising* (Muñoz Ryan 2000) was finally a story that she could connect to—one that described the experiences of her Mexican grandparents. It is especially important for struggling readers, who often are disengaged and disinterested, to find characters like themselves and events and surroundings to which they can relate. Brozo (2002) describes how a Mexican American adolescent receiving reading support made meaningful connections and developed a deep empathy with Gary Paulsen's main character, Manny Bustos, in *The Crossing*, a gripping story about a homeless fourteen-year-old boy from Juarez, Mexico, who plans to secretly cross over into El Paso, Texas, with hope for a better life.

There are many good books about strong characters with diverse backgrounds, customs, languages, and abilities that support diversity, promote understanding of multiple perspectives, and allow students to make real-life connections between themselves and the text. In some books, authors address different perspectives and social issues through the lens of several characters. For instance, in Gary Soto's realistic fiction novel *Pacific Crossing* (1993), the author explores differences in language, religion, and culture between a Mexican American teenager and the adolescent son of his host Japanese family and describes the close bond that develops between them. In Arthur Yorinks's clever fantasy picture books *Company's Coming* (1988) and *Company's Going* (2001), the author reminds us about the dangers of fearing those unlike ourselves and the benefits of understanding, appreciating, and enjoying perspectives different from our own—in this case, aliens from outer space! In other books, themes are expressed through the thoughts and actions of central characters that come from a specific culture, race, or ethnic group. For example, in Lawrence Yep's comical and warm-hearted *Cockroach Cooties* (2000) about an Asian American family, Bobby explains to his older brother, "Just because something is different doesn't make it a monster" (39). Understanding different perspectives and portraying universal feelings are paramount in Yumoto's moving novel *The Friends*, about three Japanese teenagers and a lonely old man. In *Calling the Doves* (1995), a magical picture book written in English and Spanish, Juan Felipe Herrera eloquently writes about his experience growing up with his loving parents who are migrant farm laborers, and the intangible gifts they bestow on a famous Mexican American poet. In the short eighty-nine-page novel *The Jacket* (Clements 2002), the author examines unconscious prejudices, differences, and universal human experiences through the eyes of his sixth-grade protagonist, Philip, who assumes a jacket is stolen when it is not.

Jack Gantos explores learning and behavior differences from the perspective of Joey Pigza, a sensitive, well-intentioned boy with attention deficit disorder (ADD). His books *Joey Pigza Swallowed the Key* (1998),

Joey Pigza Loses Control (2000), and *What Would Joey Do?* (2002) contain complex characters—like Joey, his grandma, and dad, who are all "wired"—in humorous and moving situations that reveal authentic thoughts and feelings. Mills writes, "Without giving Joey any compensating talent, Gantos lets us see that Joey is an absolutely terrific kid for whom life will always be a challenge" (2002, 541). In *Egg-Drop Blues* (1995), Jacqueline Turner Banks describes the strengths and challenges of an industrious sixth grader with dyslexia who tends to confuse small words, reverse numbers, and has difficulty shifting tasks. Cognitive differences are sensitively explored by Betsy Byars in *Keeper of the Doves* (2002) as Amen, the young protagonist, discovers that Mr. Tominski—the childlike keeper of the doves—can be many things depending on whose perspective was given: "How many things can one man be? Aunt Pauline said he was a drifter, a hobo. Mama called him a harmless old man. Grandmama called him a dove magician. You said he was a friend. I think he was a hero for saving your life" (p. 115).

Karen Hesse describes the impact of literacy and poverty from the perspective of Juice, the young protagonist with reading problems in her poignant novel *just Juice* (1998) about family loyalty and love. In Cynthia Rylant's moving, short novel, *A Blue-Eyed Daisy* (1985), readers will discover a sensitive, quiet eleven-year-old with the universal feelings and experiences of a young adolescent living in a large family. They will also read about class differences that make it impossible for Ellie to correct decaying teeth, to have her own bedroom, or to get more than a few cents to buy a valentine. Finally, in Andrew Clements's *The Janitor's Boy* (2000), Jack, who is viciously teased by classmates because his father is a janitor, gets "even" with his father by defacing a table and chair in the music room with wads of smelly chewing gum. When an angry vice principal assigns him to help the "head custodian" for three weeks, Jack discovers the complexities and skills required for being responsible for a building, his father's enormous role in helping others, and why the day a janitor put a broom in his father's hand was the day that saved his life (p. 137).

Ada (2003) writes that the term *multicultural* emphasizes the need to know, understand, and celebrate people of all ethnic, cultural, and linguistic origins, of all religious and sexual orientations, and of all physical and mental abilities (7). The following books represent multiple perspectives, celebrate the richness of diversity, and introduce readers to characters they can understand, relate to, and empathize with, as well as problems and events that raise social issues and generate critical discussions. Selections represent various genres as well—picture books, fantasy, and realistic and historical fiction are included in the following short synopses. All of the selections have readability levels below interest levels and present opportunities for language development, interpretation, evaluation, and appreciation and enjoyment of text. Each selection is described in more detail with accompanying discussion questions and extensions in chapter 3, Book Descriptions, Discussion, and Extensions.

CULTURAL AND RACIAL DIVERSITY

Asian and Asian American

- *Cockroach Cooties* by Lawrence Yep (2000). This witty short novel, set in Chinatown, chronicles the trials and tribulations of two brothers as they try to outsmart Arnie, the classroom bully, with a secret weapon named Hercules (Bobby's pet cockroach). Yep's book explores the importance of considering different perspectives and uses Bobby, the younger brother, as a vehicle that looks at bugs and people (e.g., Arnie) from their own point of view.
- *Hokusai: The Man Who Painted a Mountain* by Deborah Kogan Ray (2001) (picture book). Illustrated in subtle watercolors and written in fascinating, readable text, the author/illustrator tells the remarkable story about Hokusai, a famous and prolific Japanese artist from the peasant class, who changes the art of Japan and influences the Western world.
- *The Friends* by Kazumi Yumoto (printed in the United States, June 1998). This is a heart-warming novel set in Japan about change, friendship, separation, and growing up. Three twelve-year-old friends spy on a lonely old man they think is dying to try to find out what dying is like. As the boys gradually begin to care for the old man, he invites them into his life.
- *The Journal of Wong Ming-Chung: A Chinese Miner* by Laurence Yep (2000). This fascinating story is made up of journal entries from a bright and courageous twelve-year-old who leaves China in 1851 to join his uncle in the dangerous gold mines in Colorado. Yep

describes the dangers and discrimination against immigrants competing for gold and presents believable, complex characters who struggle with conflicts of nature, self, and society.

African American

- *Bad Boy: A Memoir* by Walter Dean Myers (2001). In Myers's fascinating memoir, he describes a loving family, school experiences filled with failures, a life with peers that often got him in trouble, and a love for reading that brought success, purpose, and fulfillment as a successful writer.
- *Champion: The Story of Muhammad Ali* by Jim Haskins (2002) (picture book). Illustrated with rich, realistic paintings by Eric Velasquez, this fascinating picture book describes major events in the life of Muhammad Ali that include winning three heavyweight titles, his religious beliefs and refusal to fight in Vietnam, and his triumphant lighting of the Olympic torch in 1996.
- *Coming Home: From the Life of Langston Hughes* by Floyd Cooper (1994) (picture book). This beautiful picture book focuses on the young life of the famous poet/writer and events that help to shape his later writing, such as the separation from his parents, his grandma's stories of black heroes and segregation, and the jazzy blues music of Kansas City.
- *Duke Ellington* by Andrea Davis Pinkney (1998) (picture book). Accompanied by flowing and colorful scratchboard illustrations by Brian Pinkney, this story shines with colorful language and art that capture the brilliant life and music of the "Duke," the gifted African American jazz musician whose music dazzled the Cotton Club and New York's Carnegie Hall.
- *Free at Last! The Story of Martin Luther King, Jr.* by Angela Bull (2000). This short nonfiction text is full of photographs, drawings, and sidebars that support comprehension and introduce readers to Dr. King and his life's work to ensure social justice for all Americans.
- *Freedom's Wings: Corey's Diary* by Sharon Dennie Wyeth (2001). This moving and exciting novel is written in short journal entries by the young slave Corey, who, with his mother, flees Kentucky via the Underground Railroad to find his father and freedom.

- *Handbook for Boys* by Walter Dean Myers (2002). This poignant short novel is about the changes one man (Duke Wilson) makes in the lives of two teenagers who are given the choice to either be supervised by Duke and work in his barbershop, or spend time in a juvenile detention facility. Myers writes from the perspective of sixteen-year-old Jimmy Lynch, charged with assault for losing his temper.
- *Jackson Jones and the Puddle of Thorns* by Mary Quattlebaum (1994). This short humorous chapter book describes how entrepreneurial Jackson tries to change his mother's birthday surprise—a garden plot—to his advantage and discovers that friendship and business don't mix.
- *Jackie Robinson* by Kenneth Rudeen (1974). This informative, interesting short chapter book describes the talent and challenges facing athlete Jackie Robinson, the first African American to play in the major leagues.
- *Locomotion* by Jacqueline Woodson (2003). Eleven-year-old Lonnie has discovered the power of poetry. This short novel, written in simple, moving verse from Lonnie's perspective, describes the range of feelings and experiences of the sensitive and gifted young writer.
- *Malcolm X: A Fire Burning Brightly* by Walter Dean Myers (2000) (picture book). Myers's well-written text and Leonard Jenkins's bold, realistic paintings tell the story about this complex man who fought for social justice.
- *Martin's Big Words* by Doreen Rappaport (2001) (picture book). Beautifully written and illustrated, Rappaport's text highlights Martin Luther King's life and the "big words" that promoted social justice and helped to change a nation.
- *Miracle's Boys* by Jacqueline Woodson (2000). In this sensitive, short novel about family and survival, three brothers discover their strengths and family loyalty as they struggle to stay together after the death of their parents.
- *Monster* by Walter Dean Myers (1999). This riveting novel is about Steve Harmon, a sixteen-year-old on trial for felony murder. The novel is told from Steve's perspective, alternating between his screenplay (written to distance himself from the horrific events) and actual events that occur during the trial. "Monster," a name that Steve identifies with himself, is first mentioned by the prosecutor when she describes the young offender.

- *My Man Blue* by Nikki Grimes (1999) (picture book). Free verse and rhyme accompanied by Jerome Lagarrique's dark, bold, impressionistic, acrylic paintings portray a loving, complex relationship between Damon, a schoolboy with asthma, and his mother's friend, Blue. The poet's descriptive, moving language traces the growing relationship between two sensitive people and the feelings and transformations that a caring friendship can create.
- *The Greatest Muhammad Ali* by Walter Dean Myers (2001). This biography richly describes the complex, talented African American, the choices he made, his reasons for doing so, and his lasting contributions to society.
- *The Other Side* by Jacqueline Woodson (2001) (picture book). Woodson's sensitive text, accompanied by E. B. Lewis's soft watercolors, tells about a growing friendship between two young girls in spite of the fence and racial barriers that separate them.
- *The Skin I'm In* by Sharon Flake (1998). Flake's gripping novel is about identity and the consequences of following a group of malicious peers. Written in the first person through Maleeka's perspective, Flake's complex characters include Maleeka, taunted by her peers because of her darker skin; Miss Saunders, her new white teacher who has a disfiguring skin condition; Charlese, Maleeka's tough, untrustworthy friend; and Caleb, constant in his friendship, admiration, and affection.
- *When Marian Sang* by Pam Muñoz Ryan (2002) (picture book). The elegant text complemented by realistic illustrations describes the extraordinary voice, courage, and determination of Marian Anderson to overcome obstacles of prejudice and discrimination to become recognized as one of the world's most gifted opera singers.

Latino

- *Calling the Doves* by Juan Felipe Herrera (1995) (picture book). Lyrically written in English and Spanish, the poet celebrates his Mexican heritage and describes growing up with his strong and resourceful parents (migrant workers in California) whose loving influence helped to shape his writing.
- *Frida* by Jonah Winter (2002) (picture book). Colorful, whimsical illustrations support a rich, simple text that describes the courageous

life of Frida Kahlo, a gifted Mexican painter. One to three sentences per page—often woven in with the mystical illustrations—introduce the reader to an extraordinary woman and artist.

- *It Doesn't Have to Be This Way: A Barrio Story* by Luis J. Rodriguez (1999) (picture book). The moving text, written in both Spanish and English, describes a boy's struggle to stand up to the pressures of gang membership, a near-tragic accident that occurs because of his gang involvement, and a twelve-year-old cousin and uncle who are pivotal forces in changing his life.
- *Magic Windows* by Carmen Lomas Garza (1999) (picture book). This beautiful book describes the artist's numerous paper cutouts, her creative process, and the Mexican traditions and family members that inspired many of the designs.
- *Roberto Clemente* by James Buckley Jr. (2002). This short chapter book informs baseball fans about the inspiring life of the Puerto Rican right fielder and his compassion for helping others.
- "Seventh Grade" from *Baseball in April and Other Stories* by Gary Soto (1990). In this short story from Soto's marvelous collection about young Mexican Americans, Victor tries to impress Teresa by pretending to speak French. Spanish words appear throughout Soto's stories, supporting the culture and bringing the richness of another language.
- *Sammy Sosa: Home Run Hero* by Jeff Savage (2000). Fascinating facts and color photographs span Sammy's early years as a poor, aspiring ballplayer in the Dominican Republic to his baseball fame with the Chicago Cubs and his generosity, kindness, and support for others in need.

Native American

- *The Girl Who Chased Away Sorrow: The Diary of Sarah Nita, a Navajo Girl* by Ann Turner (1999). Sarah Nita, granddaughter to Shimasani (also Sarah Nita), carefully writes down her grandmother's words as the old woman describes the Navajos' capture by American soldiers and her long walk in 1864 to Fort Sumner when she was twelve. Short, descriptive journal entries portray family loyalty, love, bravery, survival, and the rich cultural heritage of the Navajo Indians.

- *The Journal of Jesse Smoke: A Cherokee Boy* by Joseph Bruchac (1991). Jessie, a young, literate Cherokee, sensitively describes in short journal entries the two year period from 1837–1839 in which he, his family, and all Cherokee Indians were forcibly removed from their lands and homes, first to holding concentrations camps and then to Oklahoma, walking what is now known as the Trail of Tears.

LEARNING, BEHAVIORAL, AND PHYSICAL DIFFERENCES

- *Egg-Drop Blues* by Jacqueline Turner Banks (1995). Judge Jenkins must raise his grades to avoid failing science. Coercing twin brother, Jury, into entering a science rally, Judge doesn't let his reading problems (dyslexia) stop him from bringing home the prize.
- *Gathering Blue* by Lois Lowry (2000). Kira, a gifted weaver who has recently lost her mother, has become an outcast in her primitive society because of her deformed, lame leg. In the author's primitive futuristic society, others covet Kira's land and wish to ostracize her. Mysteries, secrets, rules, conformity, and danger are part of Lowry's companion novel to *The Giver*.
- *Joey Pigza Loses Control* by Jack Gantos (2000). This humorous short novel describes a likable boy with ADHD who spends the summer with his dad who tries to make him into what he is not—a baseball player who will play in the big leagues!
- *Keeper of the Doves* by Betsy Byars (2002). A short, sensitive novel set in the late 1800s and told from the perspective of young Amen (Amie) who discovers that elusive Mr. Tominski is not who he appears to be. Called a murderer by her twin sisters, the dove magician by her grandmama, and a friend and family member by her father, Amie discovers the dangers in judging people different from oneself.
- *Reach for the Moon* by Samantha Abeel (1994). This impressive book of poems, steeped in imagery and descriptive language, is written by a young thirteen-year-old poet with learning disabilities in spelling and mathematical calculation.

- *Vanishing* by Bruce Brookes (1999). This riveting short novel is about an eleven-year-old girl who quits eating so that she will "float away" from family conflicts, and a fellow patient suffering from cancer who brings her back to reality.
- *What Would Joey Do?* by Jack Gantos (2002). This time Joey must depend on himself. His father has returned on Thanksgiving to harass his mother, and his grandma is dying of emphysema. Following his grandma's advice, Joey discovers that as long as he helps himself, he will be going in the right direction (p. 227). This is a humorous and moving sequel to *Joey Pigza Loses Control*.
- *Thank you, Mr. Falker* by Patricia Polacco (1998). This autobiographical picture book by renowned author/illustrator Patricia Polacco describes her struggles in learning to read and her immense drawing talent. See also her short biography in *Authors by Request* (Campbell and Collison) that describes her learning disability with reading (dyslexia) and numbers (dysnumeria).
- *Things Not Seen* by Andrew Clements (2002). Clements writes a suspenseful story about Bobby Phillips, who wakes up one morning to discover that he is invisible. During a trip to the library, he meets and befriends Alicia Van Dorn, a blind girl, who helps him grapple with his life-changing circumstance and in the process, changes both of their lives.

CLASS DIFFERENCES

- *A Blue-Eyed Daisy* by Cynthia Rylant (2001). This lovely short novel (ninety-nine pages) describes a year in the life of a sensitive, quiet eleven-year-old, the youngest of five sisters. Ellie's father is "a drinking man" (p. 3), brought on from losing his job due to a mining accident. Rylant describes the richness of family love, friendship, and community in a setting that portrays poverty, hardships, and sacrifice.
- *just Juice* by Karen Hesse (1998). Juice, like her father, has difficulty reading words but excels at making things with her hands. The family has little income since Pa lost his mining job. As Juice exclaims, "But with Pa not working at all, life is rough as a cob"

(p. 10). This is a moving book about family strength, determination, and the impact of poverty and illiteracy.

- *Locomotion* by Jacqueline Woodson (2003). See "New Boy" (p. 29), "New Boy Poem II" (p. 41), "New Boy Poem III" (p. 72), and "New Boy Poem IV" (p. 78). In Woodson's eloquent novel written in verse, eleven-year-old Lonnie describes the "new boy" who is the object of class laughter and ridicule because of his country speech and poor dress (high-water pants, light blue socks, a white shirt buttoned all the way up, and a granddaddy country hat) (p. 29–30). Each poem provides more information about the "new boy" and the developing friendship between Lonnie and Clyde.
- *Pictures of Hollis Woods* by Patricia Reilly Giff (2002). Hollis, a lonely, artistically talented, ward of the state, is placed in numerous foster homes, only to run away to preserve her identify of being someone worthwhile when inside she feels that she is not. When she meets and comes to love Josie, a retired, eccentric art teacher, her first thoughts are for this elderly friend who is losing her memory.
- *The Janitor's Boy* by Andrew Clements (2000). Jack is embarrassed that his father is the head custodian at his school. Now in fifth grade, taunts and jeers from classmates about being the janitor's son make Jack angry with his father for the situation he is in. When Jack decides to get even by defacing a music table and chair with wads of chewing gum, his punishment is janitor duty after school to help the head custodian (who the vice principal doesn't know is Jack's father) clean up gum! Subsequent fast-moving events help Jack discover the complexities and strengths of the father he has always loved.

DIVERSE CHARACTERS AND MULTIPLE PERSPECTIVES

- *Company's Coming* by Arthur Yorinks and illustrated by David Small (1988) and *Company's Going* by Author Yorinks and illustrator David Small (2001) (picture books). The first humorous story describes Shirley and Moe, who in the midst of entertaining relatives and friends, discover aliens at their doorstep. A frightened

Moe alerts the FBI, Pentagon, Army, Air Force and Marines who swarm down on the gentle, peaceful, and gift-bearing (a blender for Shirley!) spaceman. *Company's Going* reverses the plot when Shirley and Moe return with their new friends to the aliens' planet to cater a wedding reception and find themselves the objects of fear and misunderstanding.

- *Hoot* by Carl Hiaasen (2002) (Newbery Honor) humorously describes how Roy Eberhardt, a new boy in Trace Middle School, befriends soccer star Beatrice Leep (i.e., Beatrice the Bear) and her runaway barefoot stepbrother, Napoleon Bridger (i.e., Mullet Fingers), and outsmarts class bully, Dana Matherson, to save a group of small burrowing owls. All of Hiaasen's characters come from different homes, family dynamics, and social classes.

- *Holes* by Louis Sachar (1998) (Newbery Award; National Book Award) depicts the plight of Stanley Yelnats, sent to Camp Green Lake, Texas, to dig holes (five feet deep, five feet across) for a crime he did not commit, and Hector (Zero) Zeroni, a boy who helps dig Stanley's holes in return for reading lessons. Sachar artfully weaves in events that occur a hundred years earlier with Stanley's ancestors and the curse that seems to hover over the overweight, self-deprecating teenager. Issues of race and discrimination separate Kissing Kate Barlow, the schoolteacher turned outlaw, and her lover, Sam the Onion Man. Camp Green Lake campers, like Zigzag, Armpit, X-Ray, and Magnet, come from different races and backgrounds that support these rich secondary characters.

- *Pacific Crossing* by Gary Soto (1993). This intriguing novel describes the friendship between Lincoln Mendoza, a Mexican American exchange student, and Mitsuo, the son of Mr. and Mrs. Ono, his host Japanese family. Language, religion, and cultural differences are shared between the two boys who form a friendship that extends across the Pacific.

- *Pink and Say* by Patricia Polacco (1994) (picture book). Patricia Polacco describes the strong bond between two adolescent soldiers in different Union regiments during the Civil War. Based on a factual account from an ancestor of the author, Polacco masterfully illustrates and writes about friendship and loyalty between a black and a white, the inequities of race, and the tragedies of war.

- *Stargirl* by Jerry Spinelli (2002). This is a fascinating and disturbing fantasy about one unusual teenager who is different, and another teenager who initially follows his heart and then caves in to the pressure and cruel actions of his peers. Spinelli explores the impact of peer pressure on all of his young characters and the rare occasion when one teenager stays true to herself.
- *The Jacket* by Andrew Clements (2002). Philip accuses Daniel of stealing his younger brother's jacket when he sees the fourth grader in a jacket that looks like his brother's. Daniel angrily denies Philip's accusation when the boys are brought to the principal's office. Philip soon realizes his mistake and wonders if he would have made the same accusation if Daniel had been white. Clements writes: "I wanted to write a story about that moment when unconscious prejudices rise to the surface, a story that would explore differences and emphasize our common humanity" (chapter notes).

Standards for the English language arts (NCTE and IRA) state that students should have opportunities to read a wide range of print to build understanding of themselves and cultures of the United States and the world. Tillotson writes that it is crucial for children to see themselves in literature, and that books with diverse characters and good stories should be shared with all children and used across the curriculum—not only in a multicultural unit (2003, 5). When teachers use realistic fiction books in the classroom, they support diversity, difference, and the exploration of multiple perspectives (Lewison et al. 2002, 216). Further, through facilitating critical reflection during literature discussions, teachers raise student awareness of social issues and create the potential for greater self-knowledge and social change (Silvers 2001, 562). Readers make connections with characters, settings, and themes that are familiar and they broaden perspectives when they read about cultures, values, and traditions different from their own.

REFERENCES

Ada, A. F. 2003. *A magical encounter: Latino children's literature in the classroom.* Boston, Mass.: Allyn and Bacon.

Beers, K. 2002. *When kids can't read: What teachers can do.* Portsmouth, N.H.: Heinemann.

Brozo, W. G. 2002. *To be a boy, to be a reader.* Newark, Del.: International Reading Association.

Calkins, L., K. Montgomery, and D. Santman. 1998. *A teacher's guide to standardized reading tests: Knowledge is power.* Portsmouth, N.H.: Heinemann, 59–60.

Carr, K., D. Buchanan, J. Wentz, M. Weiss, K. Brant, 2001. Not just for primary grades: A bibliography of picture books for secondary content readers. *Journal of Adolescent and Adult Literacy* 45, no. 146–52.

Fountas, I., and G. Pinnell. 1999. *Matching books to readers: Using leveled books in guided reading, K–3.* Boston, Mass.: Allyn and Bacon.

Gunning, T. 1998. *Best books for beginning readers.* Boston, Mass.: Allyn and Bacon.

Harste, J. 2003. What do we mean by literacy now? *Voices from the Middle* 10, no. 3:8–12.

Leslie, L., and J. Caldwell. 2001. *Qualitative Reading Inventory–3.* New York: Longman.

Lewison, M., C. Leland, A. Flint, and K. Möller. 2002. Dangerous discourses: Controversial books to support engagement, diversity, and democracy. *The New Advocate* 15, no. 5:215–26.

McCormick, S. 2003. *Instructing students who have literacy problems.* Upper Saddle River, N.J.: Pearson Education.

Mills, C. 2002. The portrayal of mental disability in children's literature: An ethical appraisal. *The Horn Book Magazine* (September/October): 531–42.

Silvers, P. 2001. Critical reflection in the elementary grades: A new dimension in literature discussions. *Language Arts* 78, no. 6:556–63.

Stringer, S., and B. Mollineaux. 2003. Removing the word "reluctant" from "reluctant reader." *English Journal* 92, no. 4:71–76.

Thomas, M. 2003. Teaching fantasy: Overcoming the stigma of fluff. *English Journal* 92, no. 5:60–64.

Tierney, R., and J. Readence. 2000. *Reading strategies and practices: A compendium.* Boston, Mass.: Allyn and Bacon.

Tillotson, L. 2003. What is multicultural? *Book Links* 12, no. 3:5.

Worthy, J. 2002. What makes intermediate-grade students want to read. *Reading Teacher* 56, no. 5: 568–572.

Worthy, J., and M. Sailors. 2001. "That book isn't on my level": Moving beyond text difficulty in personalizing reading choices. *The New Advocate* 14, no. 3:229–40.

2

HOW TO DEVELOP LITERACY SKILLS AND HIGHER-LEVEL THINKING

Students need to be problem solvers and critical thinkers to meet the demands of the twenty-first century. Reading standards state that students should comprehend, interpret, evaluate, and appreciate text (standards for English language arts—NCATE and IRA). Washburn-Moses (2002) recommends that special education teachers incorporate in-depth, end-of-unit assessments that encourage students to use higher-order thinking skills to address assessment standards required of all children (13). For many students with reading problems, assignments too often include filling in blanks and completing worksheets that require only factual recall. More than ever before, teachers are required to foster critical thinking skills in all readers—skills that involve making inferences, judgments, criteria for judgments (May and Rizzardi 2002, 246), and awareness of subtle biases or ethnocentric views that often permeate a text (Ada and Campoy 2004, 42).

Rankin-Erickson and Presslely's (2000) study of effective special education teachers found that literacy instruction was typically embedded in the context of real reading and writing (206) and that teachers frequently used literature and discussions about text (217). Poetry, fiction, and biography offer different avenues to literacy. Poetry is short and allows students to hear rhyming patterns, develop fluency, make inferences, and discuss descriptive language that creates images and evokes feelings.

Good fiction with well-developed characters and authentic situations facilitates meaningful dialogue that involves interpretation, analysis and evaluation, and discussion of substantive real-life issues. Kong and Fitch (2002) write that it is essential that books contain a good story so that readers have enough "stuff" to talk about (353). Autobiographies, biographies, and memoirs allow students to read about individuals who experience challenges and overcome obstacles to reach desired goals.

Reading educators emphasize the importance of building literacy skills and an enjoyment of reading through reading and discussing good books. Mingshui Cai, literacy educator and researcher, suggests that teachers ask questions that "push students to think differently," such as discussing issues about possible conflicts when two cultures meet and attitudes toward people who are different (Gandy 2003, 44–46). Ada (2003) encourages a "creative dialogue" where teachers develop conversations that use open-ended questions to foster an exchange of ideas where different alternatives are suggested and conclusions reflect the view of individual students (85). Hancock (2000) notes that critical thinking skills are promoted when readers have opportunities to interact with and discuss well-written texts with classmates. Morocco and Hindin (2002) write that students build meaningful interpretations based on analysis and argument when they read and discuss good literature with their peers. It is especially beneficial for students with reading and writing-related disabilities to have opportunities to develop skills by talking and thinking about good texts in ways that experienced readers do (Morocco and Hindin 2002, 145).

Struggling readers develop language and higher-level thinking skills when they are given explicit examples and opportunities to talk about descriptive words and figurative language, discuss and question authentic characters' conflicts and problems, and make personal connections with the text and real-life situations. A biology teacher remarked to me that if his students never hear the words, they will never learn the meaning. However, as my colleague sadly noted, it takes time to provide examples and definitions, and to discuss and apply learning, and that administrators seldom understand this. However, Fournier and Graves argue that time is wisely spent when students are engaged in higher-level, constructivist, open-ended experiences "that lead them to become creative problem solvers in the twenty-first century" (2002, 39). McCormack adds that spending time in answering two or three higher-order questions may be more useful to some students then asking them to respond to ten or more literal questions (2003, 374).

Quality children's literature that is on a student's instructional level and that is relevant and meaningful provides literacy opportunities for readers to react personally with text and affirm their roles as readers. Poetry, picture books, short chapter books, and novels provide opportunities for students to read, interpret, evaluate, reflect upon, and make connections with relevant, text-based issues and themes. Each genre provides entryways for struggling readers to develop oral language and higher-level thinking skills through a discussion format. The following examples illustrate the literacy opportunities that are inherent in quality children's literature.

POETRY AND FAIRY TALES: FLUENCY AND DISCUSSION

Poetry enriches lives and supports literacy skills. Poems contain short lines and descriptive language that promote fluency, inferential thinking, and discussion. Rhyming verse is easy to read, is often short, and contains familiar word patterns. As students read and reread poems, they become familiar with rhyming patterns and read smoother and more expressively. Brucker and Piazza (2002) note that poetry and song lyrics promote decoding and fluency in middle and secondary special education students. Poetry also requires students to look at reality in new ways (Ada 2003, 61). In the fewest of words, poets create universal feelings that provide opportunities for students to infer a poem's meaning and theme. For example, in the rhyme and free verse poems of *My Man Blue* (Grimes 1999), the poet sensitively portrays the growing friendship between a fatherless, asthmatic boy and his mother's friend, Blue. The complexities of relationships and the importance of friendship and trust are prominent themes for discussion. *The World According to Dog: Poems and Teen Voices* (Sidman 2003) contains sensitive free verse that salutes dogs through descriptive language, impressive black-and-white photographs, and teen essays about a favorite pet memory. *Hoop Queens* (Smith 2003) is full of action-packed, short, rhyming poems that describe the individual styles and talents of twelve professional basketball women. All three collections provide opportunities for students to make inferences based on information in the poet's descriptive language.

Two popular rhyming picture books for all ages by Dr. Seuss include *My Many Colored Days* (1996) and *Oh, the Places You'll Go!* (1990). The former evokes images with its splashy colors and words that portray emotions and feelings; the latter explores life's challenges and opportunities. Both rhyming texts provide opportunities for students to generate and spell rhyming patterns, develop fluency, and engage in meaningful dialogue that supports critical thinking. Shel Silverstein's popular poetry books, *Where the Sidewalk Ends* (1974), *A Light in the Attic* (1981), and *Falling Up* (1996), provide short rhymes and imaginative line drawings that illustrate both humorous and more serious themes. For example, the sensitive ten-line poem "The Little Boy and the Old Man" (*A Light in the Attic*, p. 95) examines similar life experiences that occur in old age and in the very young, such as loneliness and the inability to perform. In the short poem "No Difference," the poet ponders if conflicts will disappear if we all look the same (and God turns out the light)(*Where the Sidewalk Ends*, p. 81). Both easy-to-read poems are short and foster a critical, closer look at social issues and equity.

Lee Bennet Hopkins's collection of rhyming and free verse baseball poems, *Extra Innings: Baseball Poems* (1993), provides opportunities for meaningful discussion about sports events, such as the plight of the disliked umpire in the short poem "The Umpire." Langston Hughes's eloquent collection of poetry, *The Dream Keeper and Other Poems* (1994), contains short poems that encourage dreams, inspire hope, and celebrate individual strengths. His eight-line poem "Dreams" (p. 4) contains only thirty-two words yet evokes strong images and ideas for comparison, analysis, and reflection. *Joyful Noise: Poems for Two Voices* (Fleischman 1988) is a collection of humorous insect poems to be read by two readers. A poem is written vertically on two sides of a page and when a phrase occurs horizontally on the same line, students read together. The poems provide opportunities for choral reading—an effective activity that develops fluency through practice and reading aloud, and promotes self-esteem when students successfully read and perform in front of their peers.

Fairy tale variants have predictable language yet themes that are worth discussing for middle school readers. *The Three Little Wolves and the Big Bad Pig* (Trivizas 1997) supports discussion about power and size (the big, bad pig is a bully) and prediction and problem solving (How will the wolves outwit the pig?). *The True Story of the Three Lit-*

tle Pigs, *The Frog Prince Continued* (Scieszka), and *The Three Pigs* (Wiesner, Caldecott Medal) include repeated phrases and clever illustrations that support word identification, fluency, and reading comprehension, yet invite discussion about viewing problems and solutions from different points of view. Worthy and Prater (2002) include fairy tale variants like *The Three Little Wolves and the Big Bad Pig* and information picture storybooks, such as Jon Scieszka's *Math Curse* (1995), in their list of Readers' Theater suggestions for challenged, intermediate-age readers (296). *Math Curse* humorously asks readers to solve math problems that crop up everywhere! Reading scripts develops fluency by providing authentic opportunities for rereading and enhances self-confidence when readers practice and perform successfully (Worthy and Prater 2002, 295). Teachers can create their own Readers' Theater script by reproducing short dialogue passages (five to eight characters) or using individual picture book copies with magic markers to denote character roles (see Extensions: Drama later in this chapter).

READABLE TEXT FOR OLDER READERS

Picture books about celebrities motivate readers, include visual features that support reading comprehension (Beers 2002, 289), and provide information about ordinary people with extraordinary talents. *Champion: The Story of Muhammad Ali* (Haskins 2002) portrays major events in the famous boxer's life and includes Ali's easy-to-read short poems, depicted in bold print, that reflect his style and philosophy. *Martin's Big Words* (Rappaport 2001) includes simple language and highlights famous quotes in boldface type. Bryan Collier's striking, symbolic collages capture the meaning and impact of his "big words." Reading and discussing these two impressive picture books provided successful and motivating experiences for several discouraged teenagers with decoding problems. Both biographies have an estimated third-grade reading level (RL).

Hoops with Swoopes (2001) and *Dance!* (1998), picture books by noted photographer Susan Kuklin, capture basketball player Sheryl Swoopes dribbling or preparing for a lay-up, and choreographer/dancer Bill Jones leaping through the air or effortlessly illustrating a dance step. Both have colorful, full-size photographs, minimal text, and are about thirty-two pages in length. Biographies by Dorling Kindersley have multiple reading levels with readable text, quality photographs, and fascinating and inspiring stories such as *Roberto Clemente* (Buckley 2002), about the talented Puerto Rican right fielder whose determination and perseverance overcame poverty and discrimination to play ball. Long sentences account for the low sixth-grade reading level.

Eve Bunting's realistic fiction picture books have simple text, second- to third-grade reading levels, but social issues and themes relevant for older readers. For example, in *Gleam and Glow* (2001), Bunting creates a heartfelt and sensitive survival story about a family's escape and two goldfish that were left behind during the Bosnian war. In *One Candle* (2002), the author describes a family's traditional Hanukkah celebration of remembrance and celebration. The family watches as Grandma hollows out a potato, fills it with oil and a wick, and, with Aunt Rose by her side, tells about the dark time in Buchenwald when the two frightened teenagers stole a potato to make a candle to honor Hanukkah. Both picture books explore the darkness of war and provide rich material for exploring past events and making connections to the present. In Patricia Polacco's *Pink and Say* (1994), eloquent illustrations and text tell the moving story about two young soldiers, one black and one white, caught up in the turmoil of the Civil War. The readable picture book (third-grade RL) presents rich opportunities for discussion about issues surrounding the Civil War and race, which eventually separates the two young soldiers.

In a lighter vein, *Company's Coming* (Yorinks 1988) and *Company's Going* (Yorinks 2001), two clever picture books on the second-grade reading level, describe the humorous and insightful adventures of Bellmore couple Shirley (Shirl) and Moe when they meet, entertain, and visit aliens from outer space, and the universal feelings of suspicion of others different from ourselves. Jon Scieszka's funny, short, fantasy chapter books about the zany adventures of *The Time Warp Trio* describe the adventures of three friends who are whisked off in time by Uncle Joe's magic Book, encounter famous and dangerous people, and escape (barely!) back to the present. One eighth grader with significant reading problems was studying Egypt and King Tut. While he could not successfully read classroom material, he learned facts by reading nonfiction picture books about this period and increased fluency, vocabulary knowledge, and self-esteem by reading Scieszka's funny *Tut, Tut* about ancient Egypt, mummies, and Egyptian court intrigue. There are over twelve books in this series written on a second-grade level that are full of familiar, humorous language expressions. Some titles include *The Not-So-Jolly Roger; The Good, the Bad, and the Goofy; Tut, Tut; Knights of the Kitchen Table;* and *Sam Samurai.*

Two short chapter books with more serious themes include Cynthia Rylant's *The Heavenly Village* (1999) and *Vanishing* by Bruce Brooks (1999). *The Heavenly Village* is a short, ninety-five-page novel with moving vignettes about eight people caught between Heaven and Earth in a holding place called the Heavenly Village. With the author's simple writing style, the reader is granted a personal glimpse into the characters' strengths and weaknesses that create ties to Earth that are not ready to be broken. *Vanishing,* 101 pages, tells the riveting story about an eleven-year-old who decides to vanish, to stop eating, and to float away from her family and their problems. Brooks's vivid, descriptive language takes readers into the troubling world of his young protagonist. In *The Pictures of Hollis Woods* (2002), a little longer with 166 pages, Patricia Reilly Giff explores themes of identity, loneliness, self-worth, and talent through Hollis Woods, a sensitive, artistic, and hard-skinned eleven-year-old. Hollis is a ward of the state who has run away from numerous foster homes until she meets and comes to love Josie, a retired eccentric artist who is slowly losing her memory. *The Pictures of Hollis Woods* and *Vanishing* have third-grade reading levels, whereas *The Heavenly Village* has an estimated fifth-grade reading level. All three are appropriate for middle-school readers and present opportunities for students to make and share personal connections and discuss character perspectives and attitudes.

DESCRIPTIVE VOCABULARY AND FIGURATIVE LANGUAGE

Literacy educators Leu and Kinzer note that "literature increases vocabulary knowledge as it captures, entertains, and enriches the lives of readers with vivid experiences that are impossible to create in a classroom" (2003, 86). Instead of drilling for specific words, English teacher Amanda Otten encourages teachers to provide diverse reading opportunities for unmotivated students to discover vocabulary, while reinforcing word meaning through strategies such as making connections to real life experiences, considering multiple meanings, and using visual techniques like word maps (2003, 71). Ada writes that good literature promotes language development at any developmental age (2003, 89). There are many books that contain colorful vocabulary and figurative language that promote image making, strengthen meaning, and provide opportunities for students to develop vocabulary knowledge through self-discovery and explicit instruction.

Writers Betsy Byars, Jerry Spinelli, and Avi represent a few of the many distinctive children's authors who create rich language opportunities and interesting characters with daunting problems to solve. Betsy Byars's mystery series about the young sleuth Herculeah Jones contains vivid adjectives, verbs, and comparisons. In *Dead Letter* (1996) (third-grade RL), the author sets a suspenseful stage as Herculeah hears a crow as she is about to enter a deserted house in pursuit of a killer: "She listened as the raucous cry came again. Then there was only the rustling of the trees in the early evening breeze, a sorrowful sound, as if they mourned their fallen friends" (p. 59). Jerry Spinelli uses image-making adjectives and idioms to capture Leo's fascination with Stargirl, a tenth grader with "chocolaty eyelashes" (p. 39) and huge eyes "like deer's eyes caught in headlights" (*Stargirl* 2000, 5) (fourth-grade RL). Avi's fascinating characters and descriptive settings carry readers into believable worlds of fantasy and realism. In the fantasy novel *Ereth's Birthday*, the old porcupine Ereth is introduced in this way: "Not the sweetest smelling of creatures, Ereth had a flat face with a blunt, black nose and fierce, grizzled whiskers" (*Ereth's Birthday* 2000, 1). In the following passage from *Poppy* (1995), Avi creates an eerie setting in Dimwood Forest: "Stars glowed. Breezes full of ripe summer fragrance floated over nearby meadow and hill. Dimwood itself, veiled in darkness, lay utterly still"(*Poppy* 1995, 1). Both *Poppy* and *Ereth's Birthday* have low fourth-grade reading levels.

Lemony Snicket's clever, gloomy books about the Baudelaire orphans (*A Series of Unfortunate Events*) are full of delicious vocabulary and colorful character descriptions. For example, readers will encounter Uncle Monty's unfortunate, humorous demise early on in *The Reptile Room* (1999): "His face, usually so rosy, was very, very pale, and under his left eye were two small holes, right in a line, the sort of a mark made by the two fangs of a snake. . . . As he had promised, no harm had come to the Baudelaire orphans in the Reptile Room, but great harm had come to Uncle Monty" (p. 90). In *The Hostile Hospital* (2001), Snicket introduces the delightful adjective "spurious" followed by a contextual explanation: "Their disguise looked spurious—a word which here means "nothing like a real doctor" (p.

164) and commences to use it again and again and again ("spurious disguise," p. 174; "spurious hands," p. 178; "spurious doctors," p. 216; and "spurious intercom," p. 239)! Estimated reading levels for these sumptuous stories are sixth grade, yet Snicket's stories are favorites of middle school and junior high struggling readers. Phyllis Reynolds Naylor's clever fantasy *The Grand Escape* (1993) (low fourth-grade RL) about two bored house cats that escape to the great outdoors contains colorful descriptive words. Figure 2.1 illustrates a word map that reinforces "solitary," one of Naylor's many descriptive adjectives that artfully depicts the actions of the lovely, alluring, tabby cat Carlotta. Clip art is used in this example, along

"With a flip of her tail, Carlotta set off along the fence to continue her *solitary* prowling, while Marco and Polo thought about where they would spend the night" (p. 43).

From *The Grand Escape*, Phyllis Reynolds Naylor

Solitary (sol i tar y)
Part of Speech
adjective
Definition
Being alone
By oneself
Characteristics
Single
Lack of companions
Lonely
Lives alone

One **solitary** example was not enough for Marco.
The **solitary** cat was the only animal in the barn.
The fisherman spotted the **solitary** cat in the river.

Figure 2.1. Word Map

with the definition, part of speech, characteristics, several sentences generated by the student, and the sentence in the text.

Idioms abound in stories with readable text and provide opportunities for struggling readers to understand figures of speech that add life and color, and support characterization. For example, in *The Miserable Mill, A Series of Unfortunate Events* (2000), Lemony Snicket cleverly describes "quiet as mice" in the following manner: "The expression 'quiet as mice' is a puzzling one, because mice can often be very noisy, so people who are being quiet as mice may in fact be squeaking and scrambling around" (p. 81). In Judy Blume's funny *Double Fudge* (third-grade RL), Mr. Fargo tells Jimmy, "Guess I let the cat out of the bag" (2000, 18), Fudge repeats Grandma's expression, "You look like you just lost your best friend" (p. 24), and Jimmy compares being squeezed between strangers in a crowded subway car to "sardines in a can" (p. 49). In *Cockroach Cooties* (Yep 2000) (second-grade RL), Lawrence Yep's humorous book about two brothers and their schemes to outsmart a classroom bully, older brother Teddy describes his good-natured younger brother Bobby as always looking "at the world through rose-colored glasses" (p. 33). Gary Soto's *Pacific Crossing* (1992) (low fourth-grade RL), about two Mexican American teenagers visiting Japan in an exchange program, is full of language expressions. A few idioms and vocabulary words that confuse Lincoln Mendoza's Japanese friend include: "Blow this place," "Let's hang out," "could eat a horse," "cool," and "dude." Finally, Jury (diagnosed with dyslexia) is often confused by his twin brother's expressions in Jacqueline Turner Banks's humorous *Egg-Drop Blues* (1995) (fifth-grade RL). For example, Judge accuses Jury of "wearing his heart on his sleeve" (p. 43) and demands that his twin brother "puts money where his mouth is" (p. 55). Appendix C provides examples of idioms from children's books described in chapter 3.

Likewise, similes (comparisons with like or as) and metaphors enrich text and provide opportunities for students to make comparisons between two different objects or events. Gary Soto, noted Mexican American writer and poet, uses similes and metaphors to create lasting images. In the short story "Seventh Grade" from *Baseball in April and Other Stories* (fifth-grade RL), Victor pretends he can speak French to impress a girl in his French class. After making up words to sound French, the aspiring Romeo realizes that he has made a fool of himself.

The author uses the following metaphor to create colorful images depicting Victor's humiliation: "Great rosebushes of red bloomed on Victor's cheeks. A river of nervous sweat ran down his palms. He felt awful" (p. 57). It is easy for readers to make personal connections with pretending you are someone you are not! In the popular Newbery Honor book *Hatchet* (Paulsen 1987) (low fifth-grade RL), the author uses comparisons to evoke sensory images about his young protagonist's survival in the Canadian Northwest and "the Secret": "The MEMORY was like a knife cutting into him. Slicing deep into him with hate. The Secret" (p. 31). Hooking vivid words, images, and language comparisons to authentic characters are more meaningful than a score of workbook pages on these same skills. Good literature provides abundant learning opportunities that are especially important for struggling readers whose reading vocabulary is often hindered by limited reading experiences.

CHARACTERS AND PROBLEMS FOR CRITICAL DISCUSSION

"Books provide models of what children can do when faced with difficult life situations" (Ada 2003, 10). There are many books written on accessible readability levels for students with reading difficulties that provide three-dimensional, authentic characters engaged in a variety of conflicts involving real-life social and moral issues. Authors explore universal relationships, multiple perspectives, and social issues through real characters that we like and want to know better. The following selections are but a few that engage and motivate struggling readers as they discuss character motivations and conflicts and make meaningful connections to themselves and the real world.

Margaret Peterson Haddix challenges characters to escape situations that bind them to meaningless social mores (*Just Ella* 1999) or values and lifestyles that are built upon false premises (*Running Out of Time* 1997). Both exciting fantasies, *Just Ella* describes the entrapment of an intelligent, independent Cinderella by her powerful, shallow prince. In *Running Out of Time*, greed, lies, and seemingly easy solutions create conflict and suspense as Haddix's young heroine escapes from a contrived setting of the 1800s to the outside world of the twentieth century to find a cure for diphtheria, the disease that is ravaging her village. Both books have reading levels below interest levels: *Just Ella* has a fifth-grade reading level for sixth graders and older; *Running Out of Time* has a fourth-grade reading level for fourth through ninth graders.

Two books describe the effects of poverty on family while highlighting family loyalty and individual strengths. Karen Hesse's *Just Juice* (1998) takes place in a rural community. Jacqueline Woodson's *Miracle's Boys* (2000) takes place in a run-down apartment building near Central Park in New York. In Hesse's book, Juice is kept behind in school because the teacher says she doesn't try hard enough. As Juice says, "I am plain stupid when it comes to reading. Everybody gets it. But reading is pure torture for me" (20). Juice is not stupid, nor is her father, who hides his illiteracy and, in doing so, loses their home because of unpaid back taxes. In *Miracle's Boys,* Woodson eloquently describes the complex relationships of three brothers who have lost both parents. Tyree, the oldest at twenty-two, gives up the opportunity to go to college to support sensitive Lafayette (age twelve) and impulsive, headstrong Charlie (age fifteen). Both books provide opportunities for readers to compare and contrast characters, discuss character motivation, compare situations and events to other real-life experiences, and discuss issues surrounding social justice and equity. Both books have fourth-grade reading levels; *Just Juice* is for third through sixth grade; *Miracle's Boys* is for sixth grade and above.

Three books, *The Fighting Ground* (Avi 1984) (historical fiction), *Because of Winn-Dixie* (DiCamillo 2000), and *The Janitor's Boy* (Clements 2000) (both contemporary realistic fiction), describe rich, complex characters and multilayered themes about war, loss, love, and growing-up. In *The Fighting Ground,* Avi examines the ravaging effects of war on a young volunteer who runs away from home to fight against the British during two days in April 1778. Loyalties become blurred, the boundaries of war vague, and devastating consequences result when Jonathan follows his conscience, and in doing so, betrays his German captors to the corporal, a brash, complex leader of the American army. In *Because of Winn-Dixie,* when lonely India Opal (the preacher's daughter) rescues Winn-Dixie, a homeless mongrel with a winning smile, life changes for the fifth grader and those around her. New friends include the colorful Gloria Dump with her memory tree of hanging bottles; quiet, lonely Otis; pinched-face Amanda; and Miss Franny, the "very old, very small" (p. 40) librarian with the sweet and sorrowful Littmus Lozenge candies invented by her great-grandfather Littmus, a fourteen-year-old soldier and survivor of the Civil War. DiCamillo's moving passage describes the depth of her believable protagonist: "I lay there and thought how life was like a Littmus Lozenge, how the sweet and sad were all mixed up together and how hard it was to separate them out. It was confusing" (p. 126). Andrew Clements's *The Janitor's Boy* explores the complex relationships between father and son, the effects of war on a past generation of soldiers, and addresses questions about equality and class differences through his strong characters: Jack, a smart and sensitive fifth grader who is teased and embarrassed about his father being a school janitor (even worse, in *his* school); Jack's father, John, a head custodian and Vietnam War veteran whose life experiences have forged friendships, a compassion for those in need, and the respect of all who know him; and Jack's mother, who loves and understands both, yet feels helpless in what she calls "boy territory" (p. 51). All three books have estimated readability levels several years below interest levels (reading level high third/low fourth and interest level third though seventh grades).

Jerry Spinelli's *Stargirl* (2000) (fourth-grade RL) explores choices, consequences, and lost opportunities when Leo succumbs to peer pressure and chooses popularity over integrity, loyalty, and friendship. Andrew Clements's *The Jacket* (2002) (second-grade RL) explores hidden prejudices through the lens of his sixth-grade protagonist, Philip, who asks his mom, "How come you never told me I was prejudiced?" (p. 37). Finally, Betsy Byars, the versatile writer of easy-to-read picture books (*The Golly Sisters*), writes a beautifully crafted, short historical fiction novel *Keeper of the Doves* (high third/low fourth-grade RL). In this turn-of-the-century story, Byars explores how misconceptions and accusations result in fateful consequences for the childlike adult who keeps doves. Readers have opportunities to examine events through the attitudes of different characters, to reflect upon their own values, and to discuss social and moral issues raised in this moving and sensitive story.

Walter Dean Myers's riveting contemporary realistic fiction novel *Monster* (1999) (fourth-grade RL) is about teenager Steve Harmon who

Settings for MONSTER
starring Steve Harmon
by Walter Dean Myers

JOURNAL NOTES	SCREEN PLAY
July 7 "I hate this place!" July 8 the dream "Nobody can hear me!" July 9 the trial July 11 mama's visit July 12 arguments are over waiting for the verdict	Cell Block D Manhattan Detention Center trial--courtroom the verdict is: (GUILTY) (NOT GUILTY)

Figure 2.2. *Monster* story map—settings

is on trial for a felony murder that occurs during an attempted robbery. The story is structured around the present (Steve's trial), his journal notes, and a screenplay that Steve writes during the trial to maintain his sanity. "The film will be the story of my life. No, not my life, but of this experience. I'll write it down in the notebook they let me keep. I'll call it what the lady who is the prosecutor called me. MONSTER" (p. 5). Particularly for middle school and older students, *Monster* contains short dialogue, familiar vocabulary, and believable characters to compare and contrast, question, and analyze, and is a powerful story and theme with which to discuss and share perspectives.

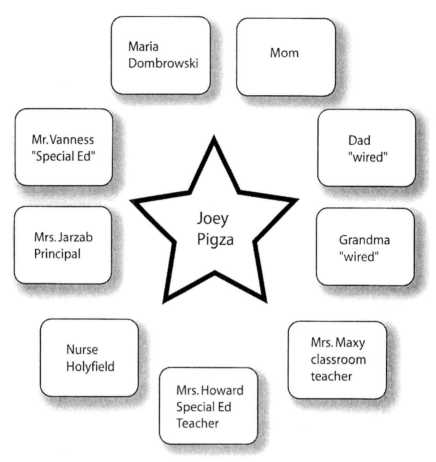

Figure 2.3. Joey Pigza story map—characters

Graphic Organizers and Discussion

Graphic organizers are effective, visual prompts that support memory and story comprehension, and facilitate opportunities for critical discussion. For example, story maps that focus on settings and events help readers remember and discuss characters' actions and motives when characters appear in different time periods, such as Louis Sachar's *Holes* (1998), which spans several generations, or in novels like Walter Dean Myers's *Monster*, whose story is told through two current settings that frame two structures with the main character having a dominant role in both. Figure 2.2 illustrates the screenplay of Myers's protagonist, Steve Harmon and

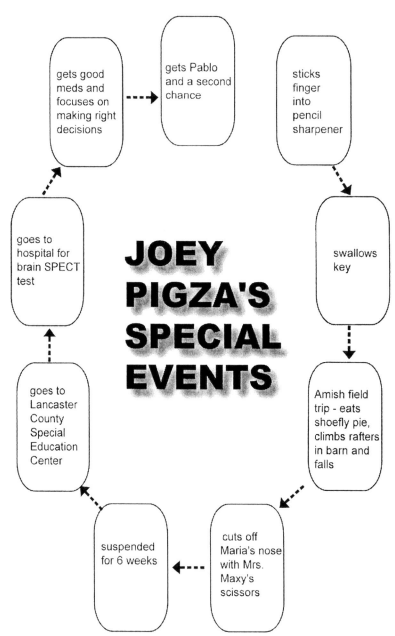

Figure 2.4. Joey Pigza's special events

**Muhammad Ali
Timeline**

1942	Born in Louisville, Kentucky
1954	Bike stolen; encouraged to learn how to fight before he found thief!
1964	Fights Sonny Liston and becomes heavyweight Champion of the World; joins Nation of Islam and becomes Muhammad Ali
1967	Refuses to fight in Vietnam; loses title and banned from boxing
1971	Five-year jail sentence reversed by Supreme Court; returns to boxing and loses title to Joe Fraiser
1974/1975	Outboxes Fraiser and wins title back from George Foreman (2nd title)
1978/1979	Loses and then wins title from Leon Spinks (3rd title)
1980/1981	Comes out of retirement to lose two bouts; suffers from brain damage; Parkinson's syndrome
1996	Carries Olympic torch in Atlanta, Georgia

Figure 2.5.   Muhammad Ali timeline

his journal notes, the two settings that provide separate structures for his gripping novel. The graphic organizer in figure 2.3 identifies the multi-layered characters in Jack Gantos's *Joey Pigza Swallowed the Key* (1998). Graphic organizers in figures 2.4 and 2.5 emphasize major events that help readers recall and sequence events during discussion. They also serve as prewriting aids to help writers remember and organize information during writing activities, such as writing a summary, a creative new chapter, or an epilogue. Students can create graphic organizers before reading (predict story events), during reading (record events as they occur), or after reading (review or summarize story).

Mathematical Extensions and Problem Solving

Good literature provides authentic situations for students to problem solve and to generate their own math problems. According to the National Council of Teachers of Mathematics (NCTM) *Principles and Standards for School Mathematics* 2000 Project, being a good problem solver can lead to great advantages; teachers can help build problem-solving skills by asking questions that help students find mathematics in their world and experience (Carpenter and Gorg 2002, 52). Some authors are obvious in devising mathematical problems for their characters to solve. For example, in the Newbery Award book *Holes* (Sachar 1998) (low fourth-grade RL), Stanley Yelnats, is sent to Camp Green Lake (a camp for delinquents) for a crime that he did not commit—stealing a pair of tennis shoes that were meant for charity. He quickly befriends Zero, who has never learned to read but is quite clever mathematically. When Stanley overhears conversation about the date being July 8, he tries to figure out how long he has been in Camp Green Lake: "I came here on May 24," he said aloud. "So that means I've been here . . . " "Forty-six days," said Zero" (p. 130). Is Zero correct? Computation (adding and subtracting) and background knowledge (knowing the number of days in May and June) are skills required to affirm Zero's conclusion. Later in the text when the two escapees eat onions to survive in the Texas desert, Stanley asks Zero how many onions they have eaten if they'd been gone a week and each had eaten about twenty onions a day. Zero quickly responds: "Two hundred and eighty onions" (p. 186). The plot and story events are full of opportunities for teachers and students to develop their own text-based math problems. Andrew Clements's heartwarming story, *The Janitor's Boy* (2000) (low fourth-grade RL), includes numerous events that invite problem solving, such as cleaning gum from X number of auditorium chairs out of a total of 855 chairs to cleaning eight tables with gum that is one-half-inch thick. In *Double Fudge* (Blume 2002) (third-grade RL), Peter visits Jimmy's loft apartment in SoHo. Jimmy proudly announces that the high ceiling is sixteen feet high and the boys commence to visualize other uses for the large space (e.g., basketball court, bowling alley, ice hockey court). What other ceilings are sixteen feet high? How high is your classroom ceiling? How can you test your predictions? Estimating, visualizing distance, and predicting are skills that naturally arise out of this simple exchange between two friends. Math educators emphasize that "problem solving can and should be used to help students develop fluency of specific skills" (Carpenter and Gorg 2000, 52). Math extensions for the above selections and more are noted in chapter 3, Book Descriptions, Discussions, and Extensions.

QUESTIONS TO PROMOTE REFLECTION AND HIGHER-LEVEL THINKING

The major goal of reading comprehension instruction should be to enable students to think about and react to what they read (Tierney and Readence

2000, 318). McCormack suggests that comprehension instruction requires time spent in the thoughtful, prolonged development of higher-level thinking skills (2003, 374). Kempe (2001) urges teachers to refine questions that help students recognize that responses to texts are not only personal but are constructed out of particular cultural contexts and to provide more opportunities for students to pose questions of their own (45, 56). Tovani (2000) asserts that readers who ask questions when they read improve their comprehension by interacting with the text, motivating themselves to read, clarifying information in the text, and inferring beyond the literal meaning (86).

Like all students, students with reading difficulties need opportunities to engage in dialogues and open-ended questions that foster reflection and higher-level thinking skills, and that validate their experiences as readers. This emphasis is not meant to exclude instruction in word identification skills. Direct instruction in phonics is essential for students who struggle with decoding; however, "the prescription for a diet heavy in phonics may detract from developing comprehension skills that encourage critical thinking and reading for meaning" (Zimmermann and Brown 2003, 604).

Frameworks and Strategies

Questioning frameworks and strategies helps teachers think about types of questions that support higher-level thinking skills and ways to promote these skills in their students. Bloom's taxonomy (1956) provides levels of questions that support higher-level thinking and includes the following hierarchical classification: knowledge, comprehension, application, analysis, synthesis, and evaluation. Questioning strategies such as the Question Answer Relationship (QAR) (Raphael 1986) help students answer types of comprehension questions by analyzing if questions require textually explicit (facts in one sentence) or implicit (information is found in several parts of the text) information, or require background knowledge (readers must use their own experiences and the text or rely solely on their own experiences). When working with struggling readers, it is important to validate background experiences. Because of reading failure and poor self-concepts, children do not trust their own background experiences and therefore don't use them (Williams and Brogan 1991, 113). The Request Procedure (Manzo 1969) encourages students to formulate their own questions through reciprocal questioning between teacher and student. The teacher and student silently read parts of a selection and then take turns asking and answering each other's questions. This strategy provides opportunities for teachers to model good questioning behavior and use questions that develop critical thinking (124–25). Further, it provides opportunities for students to *ask* questions, an important aspect of reading comprehension.

Ada and Campoy emphasize the value of discussion and write that "dialogue turns the art of reading from a passive receptive intake of information to a creative process of active engagement through questioning the text" (2004, 41). Ada's creative dialogue framework includes questions that promote understanding of text content (descriptive phrase), encourage expression of feelings and help readers relate book content to personal experiences (personal interpretative phrase), encourage reflection and support higher-order thinking skills (critical/multicultural/antibias phrase), and promote the creation of an action plan that extends text meaning (creative transformation phrase) (2004, 102–3). For example, in the creative transformation phase, students might research a topic to find out more about a particular issue, write a book, create a mural, act out a scene from a character's perspective, or write a letter to an elected official (2004, 88–89). I use critical discussion in this book to refer to discussion that presents opportunities for students to make personal connections with the story; to evaluate and reflect upon these experiences; and to examine character perspectives, attitudes, and social and moral issues in relation to their own values and beliefs.

Student Reflection

Student reflection is an important piece of reading comprehension and literature discussion. Meaningful discussions present opportunities for students to think about their own perspectives and those of their peers; to ask questions they want to know about; to share perspectives, opinions, and values; and to express personal thoughts and experiences. Group dynamics and individual tutoring situations present different opportunities for reflection. For instance, when students are in a group, it is important to reflect upon the group process. How did they feel in the group? How did the discussion go? Did they feel comfortable asking questions or sharing in the discussion? Were they active participants? Were others? Did they or others talk too little or too much? Tutorial or remediation settings present other opportunities. Students with reading difficulties often assume a passive role. They sit back and respond to teacher-directed questions, or shrug their shoulders in quiet passivity. With careful scaffolding, students learn to ask questions and assume responsibility and ownership in the reading process, and to develop confidence and a feeling of self-worth. They realize that what they think, the opinions they have, and the questions they ask are valued. Students with reading difficulties must feel invested in reading. Good literature that makes connections with students' experiences and interests provides rich opportunities to hone self-reflection and self-questioning skills.

Discussion Questions

Discussion questions follow each selection in chapter 3. Some questions are universal, such as "What did you think about the story?" "Were the characters believable?" "Did they grow and develop?" "What questions do you have about the story?" Others relate to specific vocabulary or figurative language that the author uses, or are about events, conflicts, perspectives, and social issues that naturally arise from the story's theme. For example, *The Jacket* (Clements 2002) examines racial prejudice, self-awareness, and the richness in human relationships that diversity provides. Discussion questions address the author's important theme and invite self-reflection about our own values, attitudes, and prejudices. Questions are not linear but spiral and interweave to foster a rich discussion of specific texts. Students have opportunities to relate textually explicit (facts) and implicit information, critically evaluate the story, and engage in a creative dialogue framework by making personal connections with the text and discussing and reflecting upon relevant, real-life social issues and themes. Discussion questions and extensions are followed by abbreviated descriptors (e.g., DL—descriptive language including vocabulary and figurative language) to help teachers emphasize and provide support with questions that address a particular area or individual student need. Questions and descriptors include the following:

- Recalling facts (F)
- Making predictions (P) and inferences (I)
- Understanding descriptive language (vocabulary and figurative language: similes, metaphors, idioms, and familiar expressions) (DL)
- Comparing and contrasting and evaluating story (E)
- Critically reflecting on social issues and themes (CR)
- Making personal connections (PC)
- Supporting inquiry through web-based research (R)
- Extending meaning through writing, art, drama, and mathematical problem solving (EX)
- Generating student questions (SQ)

Teachers facilitate critical discussion and support higher-level thinking skills by initiating and facilitating discussions about quality children's literature that students can successfully read, can relate to, and in which they are interested. Authentic reading experiences provide avenues for explicit instruction, guided practice, and application of skills, while promoting opportunities for students to predict, infer, critically discuss, question, and reflect upon material that is engaging and that promotes lifelong reading habits. Rather than, or in addition to, workbooks or software that include isolated sentences and paragraphs, children's literature provides cohesive, engaging stories that support literacy skills while inviting readers to personally identify with characters, consider conflicts and actions from multiple perspectives, and extend meaning through creative projects that support individual strengths. According to Ada (2003), "In the process of reading we discover things about ourselves and others that will inform, motivate, or transform our future actions. We will become more understanding, kinder, gentler, more generous, more compassionate, and more socially responsible" (15). Kempe concludes, "Students who are aware that there are choices to be made, and that there is no one natural or common sense way of reading their texts and their world, will have more textual and cultural power than would otherwise be the case" (2001, 56).

EXTENSIONS

Extensions in chapter 3 promote inquiry through research and provide opportunities for mathematical problem solving, writing, art, and drama activities that address students' talents and support reading comprehension. Students bring different strengths to reading. Howard Gardner (1983) reminds us that we all think in different ways and have various intelligences with which we solve problems. Many students with reading difficulties have artistic talents and interpret meaning through drawing, color, or design. Others write poetry or demonstrate dramatic skills. Writing, art, and drama are briefly explored to illustrate how each supports literacy skills and critical discussion and celebrates students' strengths and interests.

Writing

Writing extensions support written language skills and reading comprehension. Writing down thoughts allows students to reflect and to clarify their thinking (Tovani 2000, 19) and those thoughts do not need to be polished to serve as a starting point for discussion (Montes and Au 2003, 91). When students write responses to discussion questions, write epilogues, summaries, letters to authors, write a script to support Readers' Theater, or engage in journal writing, they are expressing thoughts in authentic situations that support literacy. Writing logs and literature response notes help to initiate discussion in literature discussion groups or grand conversations and pave the way for expressing thoughts, asking questions, and broadening perspectives through sharing and discussion.

The writing process (prewriting, drafting, revision and editing, publishing) provides structure and support for struggling readers when they write their own stories, reviews, or epilogues. It is especially important for students with reading and spelling difficulties to focus first on getting their thoughts down on paper and then organizing these thoughts before they address spelling or punctuation concerns. Publication (e.g., poems, critiques of books, epilogues) allows students to have ownership of their own writing. For example, McAlister, Nelson, and Bahr found that students with language learning disabilities especially enjoyed having ownership of their own writing and seeing it in published form after participating in a writing process instructional approach (1999, 159).

Structured writing, such as the bio-poem, provides opportunities for readers to revisit and analyze texts to discover significant information

Bio-Poem

Line 1	First name
Line 2	Three or four adjectives that describe the person
Line 3	Important relationship (e.g., daughter, father)
Line 4	Two or three things, people, or ideas that the person loved
Line 5	Three feelings the person experienced
Line 6	Three fears the person experienced
Line 7	Accomplishment
Line 8	Two or three things the person wanted to see happen or wanted to experience
Line 9	His or her residence
Line 10	Last name

Figure 2.6.   Bio-poem format

about the character: things the character loves, feelings the character experiences, fears, and accomplishments that support a complex, fully developed character. The bio-poem has several forms; one popular format is represented in figure 2.7. The acrostic (name poem) is shorter, yet provides opportunities for character description and analysis. Students use letters of the character's name as the initial letter of a word or phrase for each line. The name can be placed vertically in the middle of the poem. For example, the target letter in the name becomes part of the spelling of a word or phrase in the middle of a line. Figure 2.7 illustrates a bio-poem and acrostic poem of Joey Pigza, the young, sensitive, and "wired" protagonist in Jack Gantos's Joey Pigza books. These two activities are easily publishable on a word processor,

Joey Pigza
from
Joey Pigza Swallowed the Key

Joey
Likeable, Wired, Sensitive, Loving
Son and grandson
Loves mom and grandma
Feels afraid, different, sad
Fears the Special Ed. School, Mr. Dombrowski, failing
Accomplishes making "right decisions!"

Jittery
Trips **O**ver scissors
Cuts tip off Maria's nos**E**
Swallows ke**Y**

Figure 2.7.   Joey Pigza poems

and with illustrations such as clip art, are impressive pieces of published student work. Ada and Campoy describe writing opportunities for teachers, students, and families using the acrostic format to create books based on the features of one's name (2004, 106). When students develop a bio-poem based on research of actual people, type final copies using word processing software, and attach clip art, they connect language arts and social studies with technology (Haley and Huddleston 2003).

Finally, books provide models for the books that students write (Ada 2003, 10) and provide opportunities to use new words and descriptive language. Authors, such as Gary Paulsen, Walter Dean Myers, Jerry Spinelli, and Avi, use figurative language and colorful vocabulary to tell gripping stories. When students write book critiques, creative stories, epilogues, or future chapters about the author's characters and use similar descriptive words and language, they extend vocabulary meaning and develop expressive language skills.

Art

Like the famous illustrator and writer Patricia Polacco, students with reading difficulties frequently have artistic talent. Drawing pictures or adding brilliant splashes of color come naturally to many children who struggle with reading. Drawing main ideas and important events after reading promotes story comprehension, self-expression and sharing of perspectives. Strategies such as the Sketch-to-Stretch (Harste, Short, and Burke 1988) encourage readers to go beyond a literal understanding of the text by using crayons or markers to represent what the reading means to them and sharing their interpretations (353–56). Hibbing and Rankin-Erickson describe how struggling readers use their drawings of main events to serve as a reminder of past events and to help them make predictions about future ones (2003, 762). Drawing allows readers to share different interpretations about the text and provides opportunities to organize thinking and reread for more information (Mantione and Smead 2003, 21–22). Making puppets or a scene diorama or illustrating book covers, important chapter events, vocabulary words, and book themes are authentic ways to support learning, promote self-esteem, and value the artistic talents of students.

Drama

Students reinforce word meaning when they act out vocabulary words. Role-playing and drama activities allow students to delve into a character's thought processes and take on his or her perspective. Playing characters requires students to infer from their own decisions about how characters act in a particular situation (Mantione and Smead 2003) and compels students to consider aspects of a novel from different perspectives (Bean and Moni 2003). Acting out a scene or sharing a perspective from a particular character's point of view can be done extemporaneously or with more planning. For example, Readers' Theater is a format where students practice and read character parts from a prepared script. Students have opportunities to bring their own interpretation to characters, practice oral reading, and perform in front of their peers, especially motivating for struggling readers who have a flare and talent for acting. While scripts are available commercially, some books lend themselves to Readers' Theater, such as *Put Your Eyes Up Here and Other School Poems* (Dakos 2003) that contains several poems with character parts (see "A Gift for Ms. Roys" and "I Don't Believe in Ghosts"). Teachers may also write their own script using direct quotations and a brief narrative. Roder et al. recommends four to six pages of script typed in a 14 to16 font size with four to six roles so that students do not have long to wait for their next turn speaking (2003, 55). Students first practice reading and rereading their roles before performing in front of peers. Readers' Theater provides authentic ways for students to practice oral reading and increase fluency. For example, Roser et al. report that rereading scripts and having opportunities to get into stories of carefully selected children's literature increased reading levels, reading rate, and an increased awareness and understanding of characters in bilingual fourth-graders (2003, 58–68). Students may also write their own character narrative. After reading Betsy Byars's *Summer of the Swans* (1970), Maria extended Byars's fourteen-year-old protagonist by going beyond the given dialogue to write her own script from Sara's perspective, revealing Sara's conflicting emotions for Charlie, her younger, special-needs brother. Her emotional reading gave added meaning to the text and provided an opportunity for a quiet, sensitive student to interpret a character in her own magical way. Maria read her script, and did not have the burden of memorizing it. According to Worthy and Prater, Readers' Theater especially benefits challenged readers who are seldom given speaking parts in major dramatic productions (2002, 294). Most importantly, reading and rereading good literature provides opportunities for students to construct meaning from carefully selected texts and to develop better insights and a deeper understanding of story (Roser et al. 2003, 66).

REFERENCES

Ada, A. F. 2003. *A magical encounter: Latino children's literature in the classroom.* Boston, Mass.: Allyn and Bacon.

Ada, A. F., and F. I. Campoy. 2004. *Authors in the classroom: A transformative education process.* New York: Pearson Education, Inc.

Bean, T., and K. Moni. 2003. Developing students' critical literacy: Exploring identity construction in young adult fiction. *Journal of Adolescent and Adult Literacy* 46, no. 8: 638–48.

Beers, K. 2002. *When kids can't read: What teachers can do.* Portsmouth, N.H.: Heinemann.

Bloom, B. 1956. *Taxonomy of educational objectives, Handbook I: Cognitive domain.* New York: David McKay.

Brucker, P.O., and R. Piazza. 2002. *Today.* Reading Instruction for Older Students. 9, no. 3 (September/October): 12–13.

Carpenter, J., and S. Gorg, eds. 2002. *Principles and standards for school mathematics.* Reston, Va.: National Council of Teachers of Mathematics.

Fournier, D., and M. Graves. 2002. Scaffolding adolescents' comprehension of short stories. *Journal of Adolescent and Adult Literacy* 46, no. 1:30–39.

Gandy, S. 2002. Mingshui Cai talks about reader response. *Illinois Reading Council Journal* 30, no. 4:44–49.

Gardner, H. 1983. *Frames of mind: The theory of multiple intelligences.* New York: Basic Books.

Haley, N., and A. Huddleston. 2003. The bio-poem: Connecting language arts and social studies with technology. *Voices from the Middle* 10, no. 4:22–23.

Hancock, M. 2000. *Children, books, and teachers in K–8 classrooms.* Upper Saddle River, N.J.: Prentice-Hall.

Harste, J. C., K. G. Short, and C. Burke. 1988. *Creating classrooms for authors: The reading-writing connection.* Portsmouth, N.H.: Heinemann.

Hibbing, A. N., and J. R. Rankin-Erickson. 2003. A picture is worth a thousand words: Using visual images to improve comprehension for middle school struggling readers. *The Reading Teacher* 56, no. 8:758–69.

Kempe, A. 2001. No single meaning: Empowering students to construct socially critical readings of text. In *Critical Literacy*, edited by H. Fehring and P. Green. Newark, Del.: International Reading Association.

Kong, A., and E. Fitch. 2002. Using book clubs to engage culturally and linguistically diverse learners in reading, writing, and talking about books. *The Reading Teacher* 56, no. 4:352–62.

Leu, D., Jr., and C. Kinzer. 2003. *Effective literacy instruction, implementing best practice.* 5th ed. Upper Saddle River, N.J.: Merrill, Prentice Hall.

Mantione, R., and S. Smead. 2003. *Weaving through words: Using the arts to teach reading comprehension strategies.* Newark, Del.: International Reading Association.

Manzo, A.V. 1969. The request procedure. *Journal of Reading* 12: 123–26.

May, F., and L. Rizzardi. 2002. *Reading as communication.* 6th ed., Upper Saddle River, N.J.: Pearson Education.

McAlister, K., N. Nelson, and C. Bahr. 1999. Perceptions of students with language and learning disabilities about writing process instruction. *Learning Disabilities Research and Practice* 14, no. 3:159–72.

McCormack, S. 2003. *Instructing students who have literacy problems.* 4th ed. Upper Saddle River, N.J.: Merrill Prentice Hall

Montes, T., and K. Au. 2003. Book club in a fourth-grade classroom: Issues of ownership and response. In *After early intervention, then what? Teaching struggling readers in grades 3 and beyond*, edited by R. McCormack and J. Paratore, 70–93. Newark, Del.: International Reading Association.

Morocco, C., and A. Hindin. 2002. The role of conversation in a thematic understanding of literature. *Learning Disabilities Research and Practice* 17, no. 3:144–59.

Otten, A. 2003. Defining moment: Teaching vocabulary to unmotivated students. *English Journal* 92, no. 6:75–78.

Rankin-Erickson, J., and M. Pressley. 2000. A survey of instructional practices of special education teachers nominated as effective teachers of literacy. *Learning Disabilities Research and Practice* 15, no. 4:206–23.

Raphael, T. 1986. Teaching question-answer relationship, revisited. *The Reading Teacher* 39, no. 6:516–22.

Roser, N., L. May, M. Martinez, S. Keehn, J. Harmon, and S. O'Neal. 2003. Stepping into characters: Using Readers' Theater with bilingual fourth graders. In *After early intervention, then what? Teaching struggling readers in grades 3 and beyond*, edited by R. McCormack and J. Paratore, 40–69. Newark, Del.: International Reading Association.

Shanker, J., and E. Ekwall. 2003. *Locating and correcting reading difficulties.* Upper Saddle River, N.J.: Merrill Prentice-Hall.

Tierney, R. J., and J. E. Readence. 2000. *Reading strategies and practices.* Needham Heights, Mass.: Allyn and Bacon.

Tovani, C. 2000. *I read it, but I don't get it: Comprehension strategies for adolescent readers.* Portland, Me.: Stenhouse.

Washburn-Moses, L. 2002. What every special educator should know about high-stakes testing. *Council for Exceptional Children* 35, no. 4:12–15.

Williams, N., and M. Brogan. 1991. *Developing literacy in at-risk readers.* Springfield, Ill.: Charles C. Thomas.

Worthy, J., and K. Prater. 2002. "I thought about it all night": Readers' Theatre for reading fluency and motivation. *The Reading Teacher* 56, no. 3:294–97.

Zimmermann, J., and C. Brown. 2003. Let them eat more than phonics. *Phi Delta Kappan* 84, no. 8:603–5.

Children's Books

Avi. 2000. *Ereth's birthday.* New York: HarperTrophy.

———. 1995. *Poppy.* New York: Avon Books.

———. 1984. *The fighting ground.* New York: HarperCollins.

Blume, J. 2002. *Double fudge.* New York: Penguin Putnam.

Brooks, B. 1999. *Vanishing.* New York: HarperCollins.

———. 2002. *One candle.* New York: HarperCollins.

Bunting, E. 2001. *Gleam and glow.* New York: Harcourt.

Byars, B. 1996. *Herculeah Jones.* New York: Penguin Group.

Clements, A. 2002. *The jacket.* New York: Simon and Schuster.

———. 2000. *The janitor's boy.* New York: Simon and Schuster.

Dakos, K. 2003. *Put your eyes up here and other school poems.* New York: Simon and Schuster.

DiCamillo, K. 2000. *Because of Winn-Dixie.* Cambridge, Mass.: Candlewick Press.

Fleischman, P. 1988. *Joyful noise: Poems for two voices.* New York: Harper and Row.

Grimes, N. 1999. *My man Blue.* New York: Penguin Putnam.

Haskins, J. 2002. *The story of Muhammad Ali.* New York: Walker.

Hesse, K. 1998. *just Juice.* New York: Scholastic.

Jones, B., and S. Kuklin. 1998. *Dance.* New York: Hyperion Books.

Kuklin, S. 2001. *Hoops with Swoopes.* New York: Hyperion Books.

Myers, W.D. 1999. *Monster.* New York: HarperCollins.

Naylor, P. 1993. *The grand escape.* New York: Bantam Doubleday Dell.

Polacco, P. 1994. *Pink and Say.* New York: Putnam and Grosset Group.

Rappaport, D. 2001. *Martin's big words.* New York: Hyperion Books.

Rylant, C. 1999. *The heavenly village*. New York: Scholastic.

Sachar, L. 1998. *Holes*. New York: Farrar, Straus and Giroux.

Scieszka, J. 1991. *The Frog Prince continued*. New York: Viking.

———. 2002. *Hey kid, want to build a bridge? Time warp trio*. New York: Viking.

———. 1995. *Math curse*. New York: Viking.

———. 1989. *The true story of the 3 little pigs*. New York: Viking.

———. 1995. *A light in the attic*. New York: HarperCollins.

Silverstein, S. 1974. *Where the sidewalk ends*. New York: HarperCollins.

Smith, Jr., Charles. 2003. *Hoop queens*. Cambridge, Mass.: Candlewick Press.

Snicket, L. 2001. *The hostile hospital: A series of unfortunate events*. New York: HarperCollins.

———. 2000. *The miserable mill: A series of unfortunate events*. New York: HarperCollins.

———. 1999. *The reptile room: A series of unfortunate events*. New York: HarperCollins.

Spinelli, J. 2000. *Stargirl*. New York: Knopf.

———. 1993. *Pacific crossing*. New York: Harcourt.

Soto, G. 1990. *Baseball in April and other stories*. New York: Harcourt, Inc.

Trivizas, E. 1997. *The three little wolves and the big bad pig*. New York: Simon and Schuster.

Wiesner, D. 2001. *The three pigs*. New York: Clarion Books.

Yep, L. 2000. *Cockroach cooties*. New York: Hyperion.

Yorinks, A. 1988. *Company's coming*. New York: Hyperion.

———. 2001. *Company's going*. New York: Hyperion.

③

BOOK DESCRIPTIONS, DISCUSSIONS, AND EXTENSIONS

Children's books are categorized in this chapter by genre and interest. Literature descriptions include title, author, publisher, a short synopsis, estimated reading level (RL), interest level (IL), and the number of pages of text. Discussion questions provide opportunities for students to ask questions, talk about descriptive vocabulary and figurative language, make personal connections with text, locate facts, make inferences and predictions, compare and contrast, create and solve text-related mathematical problems, and promote an active, engaged discussion and critical analysis of the story and important issues raised in the text. Questions are not linear but spiral to facilitate in-depth, meaningful discussions. Whereas making predictions and inferences, comparing and contrasting, and evaluating story elements involve higher-level thinking skills, examining social issues raised in the text and reflecting on character actions, attitudes, and perspectives in relation to one's own belief system and values require a critical look at ourselves and society. Extensions provide opportunities for mathematical problem solving, and support and extend text meaning through inquiry and research, writing, art, and drama.

Five to eight discussion questions and activities follow each selection and represent examples of questions and extensions that promote meaningful discussions through student reflection, inquiry, and higher-level thinking. Specific descriptors include student-generated questions (SQ); discussing and using descriptive language, such as vocabulary, idioms, similes, and metaphors (DL); recalling facts (F); making predictions (P) and inferences (I); making personal connections (PC); evaluating story elements and comparing and contrasting characters and themes (E); critically reflecting on perspectives, attitudes, and social issues raised in text (CR); promoting inquiry through web-based research (R); and creating extensions that support mathematical problem solving, writing, art, and drama (EX). Selections do not include all ten descriptors. Rather, questions are based on the nature of the text and provide teachers with examples to facilitate student reflection and meaningful classroom discussion. For example, some selections include several examples from the same category (e.g., two questions pertaining to vocabulary or figurative language/descriptive language) or descriptors from several different categories (e.g., questions that support making inferences, personal connections, and evaluating the story). Most importantly, literature selections represent a variety of reading levels, interests, and background experiences, and motivate struggling readers to become actively involved in and to enjoy reading and talking about good books.

NONFICTION

Athletes/Sports

Hoops with Swoopes by Susan Kuklin with Sheryl Swoopes (2001). New York: Jump at the Sun, Hyperion Books for Children. Full-page action photographs and single words, short phrases, and sentences describe the WNBA champion Sheryl Swoopes as she catches, passes, shoots, blocks, and scores baskets. This picture book, containing approximately thirteen sentences, will motivate readers interested in basketball or photography.

RL: NA; IL: all ages; 30 pages

Discussion and Extensions:

- Reread the book. Make a list of action words; Write short sentences using these words (verbs) to accompany the photographs. (DL)
- Write and illustrate words that rhyme with the following: hoops, jump, bounce, pass, team. (DL)

- Look at the photographs and make up your own story about Sheryl Swoopes. Type a draft on the computer; revise and illustrate it with clip art. (EX)
- Make an acrostic poem using "SHERYL." Type it on the computer. (EX)
- Research the basketball player on the web. What else has she done? How did she begin her career? What obstacles did she face? (R)
- What questions would you like to ask her? (SQ)
- Compare Sheryl Swoopes with another famous basketball player (e.g., Michael Jordan). What are the similarities and what are the differences? (E)

Jackie Robinson by Kenneth Rudeen (1974). New York: Harper Trophy, a division of HarperCollins. This is a short chapter book about the courageous life, talent, and integrity of Jackie Robinson, the first African American to play in the major leagues. Beginning with Jackie's youth as the youngest son of a sharecropper, the author describes the second baseman's journey to become a valued player of the Brooklyn Dodgers.

RL: 2.9; IL: third to fifth grades; 53 pages

Discussion and Extensions:

- What problems did Jackie face when he accepted Branch Rickey's offer to play for the Brooklyn Dodgers? (F) Would he have the same problems today? Do racial differences affect one's ability to get a job, play baseball, or receive service? (CR)
- Why was Jackie court-martialed when he was a lieutenant in the army? (F) What do you think about his actions and the bus driver's behavior? Would Jackie be arrested today for the same offense? (CR)
- Why is Jackie Robinson considered to be a hero and great man? What did he do in 1947 (p. 3) and in 1962 (p. 50) that was extraordinary? (F) How did he help change the sport of baseball? (I)
- Compare Jackie Robinson to another great ball player. What are the similarities and differences? (E)
- If you were interviewing Jackie Robinson, what questions would you ask him? (SQ)

Lou Gehrig: The Luckiest Man by David Adler (1997). San Diego, Calif.: Harcourt Brace. Bold illustrations and fascinating, readable text depict the life of famous New York Yankee Lou Gehrig. Beginning in 1903 with Gehrig's birth and continuing through the Yankee's impressive baseball career, the author describes the athlete's talent, humbleness, and sportsmanship, his bravery during his devastating illness, and his loyalty to his teammates and fans.

> RL: fourth grade; IL: third through eighth grade; 27 pages

Discussion and Extensions:

- Lou Gehrig was born in 1903. What other important events happened that year? (F)
- In 1934, Lou Gehrig was voted into the Baseball Hall of Fame and the Yankees retired his uniform. What does that mean (retired his uniform) and why was it an important event? (I)
- What personal characteristics made Lou Gehrig a great ball player? (I) What do you like about Lou? Does he remind you of anyone you know? (PC)
- Why was Lou Gehrig loved by the Yankee players and fans? (F) Would he be just as famous today? Why or why not? (CR)
- How do you feel about the illustrations? Talk about the colors, shapes, and how the artist represents Lou and other characters. (E)
- Compare Lou Gehrig to another famous baseball player. What are the similarities and differences (e.g., baseball accomplishments, personalities)? (E)
- How did you like the story? Do you think the information was accurate? Did the author supply notes or references? (E)

> RL: low sixth grade (long sentences); IL: all ages; 48 pages, including glossary

Roberto Clemente by James Buckley Jr. (2002). London: Dorling Kindersley (Dorling Kindersley Readers, Level 3–Reading Alone). Color photographs and large, readable print tell the inspiring story of Puerto Rican right fielder Roberto Clemente, his extraordinary talent, character, and compassion for helping others.

Discussion and Extensions:

- Why is Roberto Clemente considered a hero? (I)
- Why did Bowie Kuhn say, "He had about him a touch of royalty" (p. 45)? (I)
- Do you think Roberto would receive the same "racist, second-rate treatment" (p. 30) today? Why or why not? (CR)
- Describe Roberto's accomplishments and contributions. (F)
- What did you like the most about the chapter book? The least? (E)
- Roberto was the first Latin American player to be elected to the Baseball Hall of Fame. Look on the Internet and see how many other Latin American players have achieved this distinction. (R)
- Use the following dates and make a time line of important events: 1934, 1954, 1955, 1963, 1971, 1972. (F) Illustrate the event that you think is the most important. (EX)
- What questions do you have about the book or the ballplayer? (SQ)

Sammy Sosa: Home Run Hero by Jeff Salvage (2000). Minneapolis, Minn.: Lerner Publication. Salvage's fascinating biography describes how Sammy, fifth of seven children, learned to play

> RL: middle sixth grade; IL: third grade and up; 61 pages, including the glossary

ball hitting a wadded-up sock in the Dominican Republic, and through hard work and talent, became a hero in the Dominican Republic and in the United States. Colorful photographs accompany the biography and highlight Sosa's rise to fame and his generosity to those in need.

Discussion and Extensions:

- Why is Sammy Sosa considered a hero to people of all races? (I)
- Name some challenges and obstacles that Sammy faced growing up and playing in the minor and major leagues. How did he face them? What did he do? (F) Would he face the same challenges and obstacles today in the Dominican Republic? In the United States? Why or why not? (CR)
- Name five adjectives that characterize Sammy Sosa. (DL) Use this information to write an acrostic poem about SAMMY. (EX)
- Sammy was asked if he felt pressure to beat Mark McGwire. He said that he only felt pressure being a shoeshine boy (p. 51). What did he mean? (I)
- Research Sammy's batting average on the Internet. Find out on

what date he made 500 home runs. (See *Chicago Tribune*, April 5, 2003) (R)

- The definition for a batting average is the number of hits (a batter gets) divided by the batter's official times at bat, carried to three decimal places. What would be Sammy's batting average if he gets thirty hits in ninety bats (p. 60)? Make up another problem using the facts in the book. (EX)
- What questions would you like to ask Sammy? Write to him at the following address: Sammy Sosa, c/o Chicago Cubs, 1060 West Addison Street, Chicago, IL 60613-4397. (SQ) (EX)

Shooting for the Moon: The Amazing Life and Times of Annie Oakley by Stephen Krensky (2001). New York: Melanie Kroupa Books, Farrar, Straus and Giroux. Told in readable text and expressive paintings, the author and illustrator describe the poverty, abuse, true grit, and talent of this impressive sharpshooter and rider. For example, attempting to bring food to her widowed mother and six siblings, eight-year-old Annie loaded her father's large rifle and shot her first rabbit, breaking her nose but killing the rabbit! At ten, Annie was hired to keep house for a cou-

> RL: high third grade/low fourth grade; IL: all ages; 29 pages

ple with young children, and, after two years of backbreaking labor and abuse, Annie ran away and returned home. Determined to support her family, fifteen-year-old Annie invested in traps, shot game, and sold her bounty to owners of a grocery store who, in turn, sold it to elegant restaurants. At twenty, she outshot famed sharpshooter Frank Butler, a well-known professional whom she later married. According to Annie, "Aim at a high mark and you will hit" (p. 27).

Discussion and Extensions:

- Would a sharpshooter like Annie Oakley be famous today? Would it matter that she was a female? Would she face the same obstacles (poverty, abuse) that she did in 1865? (CR)
- What personal characteristics helped Annie be successful? (I) Do you know anyone like Annie Oakley? (PC)
- What did you think about the story? The illustrations? (E)
- Are all perspectives represented in the story? Did the author present perspectives of white settlers and Native Americans such as

Sitting Bull? (CR) Write a short story about Annie from Sitting Bull's point of view. (EX)
- Make a timeline that includes five important events in Annie's life and create a simple drawing or symbol to illustrate each event on your timeline. (F)
- Look up Annie Oakley on the Internet. What new facts can you discover? (R)
- What questions do you have? (SQ)

Fine Arts: Dance, Music, Art

Dance by Bill T. Jones and Susan Kuklin (1998). New York: Hyperion Books for Children. Full-page photographs and simple sentences (approximately twelve in the book) describe the movements of dancer/choreographer Bill Jones and the effort and art that go into dance.

> RL: NA; IL: all ages; 30 pages

Discussion and Extensions:

- Look at the photographs and describe Bill Jones using five adjectives. (DL)
- List five emotions that the dancer portrays. (DL)
- Compare dancing to another sport. What are similarities? Differences? Compare Bill Jones to another athlete. (E)
- Write an acrostic poem describing BILL or DANCE. (EX)
- Make your own book. Photograph someone practicing for a performance or sports event (e.g., dancer, basketball player, musician) and write short sentences describing your photographs. (EX)
- How does dancing make you feel? (PC)
- What questions would you like to ask Bill Jones? (SQ)

Duke Ellington by Andrea Davis Pinkney, illustrations by Brian Pinkney (1998) (Caldecott Honor). New York: Hyperion Books for Children. Colorful illustrations and text describe the magic of Duke Ellington and his rise to fame, from disliking to practice piano to performing at the Cotton Club and Carnegie Hall.

> RL: low third grade; IL: third through sixth grade; 30 pages, including author's notes and sources

Descriptive vocabulary and figurative language make the picture book dazzle with the times and the tunes of the "Duke."

Discussion and Extensions:

- The author describes Duke Ellington's fingers as riding the piano keys (p. 5). What did the author mean? To what does she compare the piano? Draw a picture illustrating the Duke riding the piano keys. (DL)
- The Duke encouraged his musicians to "improvise" their solos. What did he mean? Have you ever improvised? Look up the word in a dictionary. Create a word map that includes the definition, examples, the sentence in the text, and your own sentence. Draw or act out this word. (DL)
- Where and when was Duke Ellington born? (F) How old would he be today? (EX)
- What do you think about the illustrations, the artist's technique, color, and style? Do the illustrations help the story? In what way? (E)
- Listen to a record of Duke Ellington. Use paints, crayons, or chalk and illustrate how the music makes you feel. (EX)

Frida by Jonah Winter (2002). New York: Arthur A. Levin Books, an imprint of Scholastic Press. Bold, imaginative illustrations and a short magical text describe the life of Mexican painter Frida Kahlo. Beginning with Frida's birth, Winter describes her early illness and later accident that en-

> RL: third grade; IL: second grade and up; 28 pages including author's notes

couraged a bedridden Frida to paint and depend upon art. The author's notes describe her illness with polio at age seven, her accident at age eighteen, and the influential artist and role model she was to become.

Discussion and Extensions:

- What do you think about the illustrations? Talk about the colors and shapes. How do they help tell the author's story? (E)
- Find out all you can about Frida Kahlo on the web. Where can you see her paintings? (R) Why did the author say that Frida was a role model for women? (I)
- What did art mean to Frida? Why was it so important to her? (I) Do you have a hobby, sport, or special talent that is important to you? (PC)

- Read the author's notes. Polio caused Frida to be confined to bed for months when she was young. What is polio? Is it still considered dangerous? What other famous individuals had this disease? Look on the web for more information. (R)
- How did Frida's father influence her art career? How did her health affect her art? (I)
- The author writes that Frida is known for her strength, courage, and pizzazz (p. 28). Why did she say this? Talk about what each word means and give an example of Frida's strength, courage, and pizzazz. (DL)
- Compare Frida to another Mexican, African, or European painter. How are their paintings (style, color, design) alike and how are they different? (E)

Hokusai: The Man Who Painted Mountains by Deborah Kogan Ray (2001). New York: Frances Foster Books, Farrar, Straus and Giroux. Beautifully illustrated and written text by Deborah Kogan Ray describes the genius of Hokusai, a gifted Japanese artist who rose from a poor peasant background to paint over 30,000 works of art. His masterpiece, *Thirty-six Views of Mount Fuji*, was completed when he was over seventy years old. Orphaned

> RL: fifth grade; IL: third grade and up; 30 pages, with author's notes and sources

as a child, Ray describes his love of art and rise to fame in the court, and his decline in popularity when he departed from the accepted Japanese tradition to use new styles and techniques.

Discussion and Extensions:

- Look at the illustrations. What do you think about them? Do they provide information about the Japanese culture? What do you think about the story? (E)
- Hokusai painted for the shogun and his court. What does "shogun" mean? (F)
- How did Hokusai teach himself to draw? (F)
- At eighteen years of age, Hokusai studied with a great artist and became an artist of "the floating world." What does this term mean? (DL)
- How did Hokusai's paintings change after he saw paintings from European artists? Why did Japanese patrons dislike him? (F)

- Hokusai was always poor. Why? What career choices did he make that affected his income? (F) Would you have made the same choices? (PC) Do you think that he would be as famous today if he painted the way others wanted him to paint? Why? (CR)
- Compare Hokusai with another artist that you like (e.g., the Mexican artist Frida). What are the similarities and differences in color, style, and technique? (E)
- What questions do you have about Hokusai? What would you like to ask him? (SQ)

Magic Windows by Carmen Lomas Garza (1999). San Francisco, Calif.: Children's Book Press. The artist describes fifteen delicate cut-paper murals that she calls Magic Windows; "When you look through them, you can see into another world" (p. 2). Learning the ancient craft from her grandmother in Mexico, the artist includes full-page paper cutouts and descriptions (written both in English and Spanish) that inform readers

> RL: fourth grade; IL: all ages; 31 pages

about Mexican culture. Intricate cutouts such as her grandfather's hands cutting a nopal cactus, her mother's hands rolling a tortilla, humming birds and cactus flowers, and a close-up of a Mexican dancer are displayed on backgrounds of beautiful, bold color.

Discussion and Extensions:

- Why is paper cutting so difficult? What keeps the design from falling apart (p. 4)? (F)
- What did you learn about the artist through her paper cuts? (F)
- Think of an everyday object or event in your home and illustrate it. Then use the design as a paper-cut. (EX)
- Look at Garza's cutout of hummingbirds (p. 17). What did people in ancient Mexico believe about hummingbirds? Look at the deer cutout (p. 21). What does Mexican legend say about corn? (F)
- What other countries are known for their paper cutouts? Look on the web and find out! (R) Compare Mexican paper cutouts to other cutouts (e.g., Chinese). How are they similar? How do they differ? (E)
- What would you like to ask Carmen Garza? What questions do you have about her paper-cuts? (SQ)

Thank you, Mr. Falker by Patricia Polacco (1998). New York: Philomel Books. This autobiography describes the author's struggles with a learning disability (dyslexia) and her enormous drawing talent, both discovered by a caring fifth-grade teacher. Colorful expression-

> RL: middle third grade;
> IL: third through
> seventh grade; 35 pages

istic drawings reflect Polacco's drawing talent and emotionally capture her humiliation when asked to read aloud.

Discussion and Extensions:

- How did the author react to teasing and being called names? (F) What would you have done if you were she? What would you have done if you were part of the group that teased Trisha? (PC)
- Have you ever felt like the author? Write about your feelings. (PC)
- What questions would you like to ask Patricia Polacco? Write to her on the following website: http://www.patraiciapolacco.com. (SQ) (EX)
- What were Patricia Polacco's strengths? (F) What are your strengths? (PC)
- Why was Mr. Falker a special teacher? (I) Does he remind you of anyone? (PC)
- Why do you think Eric acted the way he did? Why was he so mean to Trisha? Tell his story. (CR) Predict what he is like a year from now. (P)
- What do you think about the author's illustrations? What do you like about them? Look at another picture book and compare the illustrations. What makes Polacco's unique? (E)

When Marian Sang by Pam Muñoz Ryan (2002). New York: Scholastic Press. Moving, emotional text that includes verses from spirituals and detailed sepia-tone illustrations describe the rich talent, courage, and determination of this famous American opera singer during pre–Civil Rights America. From singing in the Union Baptist Church choir in South Philadelphia to her debut with the Metropolitan Opera, the writer shares

> RL: sixth
> grade; IL: all
> ages; 32 pages

extraordinary events in the life of this great American. Extensive notes and historical sources follow this rich story. To accompany this fine book, see *Marian Anderson: The Story of the Voice that Broke Barriers* by Kultur (www.kulturvideo.com), an informative and moving video documentary that highlights historic events in Anderson's life.

Discussion and Extensions:

- What did you learn about Marian Anderson? (F)
- What obstacles and challenges did she face? (F) Would she face the same obstacles today? Could she take singing lessons wherever she wished? Could she perform anywhere she liked? Would she be famous today? (CR)
- Marian Anderson was born in 1897. How old would she be today? (EX)
- Make a time line and highlight five important events in Marian Anderson's life. (F)
- Describe Marian Anderson. What personal characteristics (adjectives) would you use? Make a collage out of words you find in magazines (adjectives) and colors that describe her style and singing. (DL)
- Write an acrostic poem using MARIAN. Publish it on the computer and illustrate it either with muted colors (like the illustrator) or with clip art. (EX)

Leaders of Social Justice

Champion: The Story of Muhammad Ali by Jim Haskins (2002). New York: Walker. Realistic paintings and readable text that includes Ali's poems (in bold font) describe major events in his extraordinary life. Beginning with Muhammad Ali's birth, Haskins' describes his rise to fame, the winning of three heavyweight titles, his religious faith and refusal to fight in Vietnam, and finally the lighting of the Olympic torch in 1996.

> RL: high third/low fourth grades; IL: through eighth grade; 32 pages, including chronology and selected bibliography

Discussion and Extensions:

- Use the following dates and describe major events that framed Ali's life and boxing career: 1942, 1954, 1964, 1967, 1971, 1974/75, 1978, 1980/81, 1996. (F)
- How many times was Muhammad Ali heavyweight champion? (F)

- Ali would not join the army to fight in Vietnam because of his religious beliefs. What consequences resulted from this decision? (F) Would Ali face the same consequences today? Why do you think so? (CR) What would you have done? (PC)
- Describe Ali's strengths and weaknesses? (F) How did his strengths and weaknesses affect his career? (I)
- Ali came out of retirement in 1980–1981. What were the consequences of this decision? (F) Why did he make this decision? (I) What would you have done in his place? (PC)
- Cassius was born in 1942. His bike was stolen when he was twelve years old. What year did that event occur? What mathematical process did you use? (EX) How did this event affect his decision to become a boxer? (F)
- Use crayons to illustrate the theme and your feelings about the book. (EX)
- You are interviewing guests on a talk show. What questions will you ask Muhammad Ali (SQ)?

Free at Last! The Story of Martin Luther King, Jr. by Angela Bull (2000). London: Dorling Kindersley Readers. Short, nonfiction text with large type, six short chapters, photographs, drawings, and sidebars chronicle important events and people in Dr. King's life, such as the Montgomery bus boycott, the "I have a dream" speech, the Nobel Peace Prize, and his tragic death in 1968.

> RL: high third/low fourth grade; IL: third through sixth grade; 47 pages

Discussion and Extensions:

- Who was Mahatma Gandhi and how did he influence Martin Luther King, Jr.? (F)
- Why was there a bus boycott in Montgomery? What was the result of this boycott? (F)
- Why did some Americans (black and white) oppose Dr. King? (I)
- What were Dr. King's beliefs? (F) What laws or behaviors do you think he helped to change? (CR)
- If Dr. King were alive today, what would he be doing? What would he think of events around him? (P) Would he face the same obstacles and problems today as he did when he was alive? (CR)

- What would you ask him if he were in the room? (SQ)
- Research Dr. King and Mahatma Gandhi on the Internet. How were they alike? How were they different? (E) (R)

Malcolm X: A Fire Burning Brightly by Walter Dean Myers (2000). New York: HarperCollins. Clear, readable text and realistic paintings describe a complex man, his turbulent life, and his fight for social justice. Myers intersperses boldface quotes from Malcolm X with a fascinating narrative that depicts family relations and subsequent events that helped to shape his short life and contributions.

> RL: sixth grade; IL: all ages; 32 pages

Discussion and Extensions:

- What did you learn about Malcolm X that you did not already know? (F)
- What were Malcolm's strengths and his weaknesses? (F)
- Why did Malcolm's English teacher discourage him from becoming a lawyer? (I) Do you think that he would be treated the same way today? Why or why not? (CR)
- What would you have done in a similar situation if someone told you that you could not attain your goal? (PC)
- Compare Malcolm X to Martin Luther King Jr. How were they alike and how were they different? How did they promote social justice? (E)
- Look at the chronology of events following the biography. What questions would you like to ask Malcolm about his life? (SQ)
- What did you like about the book? How do you feel about the illustrations? Which illustration is your favorite? Why? (E)

Martin's Big Words by Doreen Rappaport (2001). New York: Hyperion Books for Children. Simple language and quotes in boldface highlight important events in Dr. King's life and the message that helped to change a nation. Equally impressive are Bryan Collier's symbolic paintings made from watercolor and cut-paper collage that support and extend Rappaport's text. A timeline of important events and websites follow the text.

> RL: high third/low fourth grade; IL: all ages; 29 pages

Discussion and Extensions:

- What did you learn about Martin Luther King Jr.? (F)
- Why did the artist use stained-glass windows throughout the story? (Read author's notes) (F). How do you feel about the illustrations? What illustration is your favorite? Are their any illustrations that you don't like? (E)
- Why do you think the illustrator used the signs "inside" "outside" on the bus windows? Could he use them today? Do similar conditions exist today? (CR)
- What happened in Montgomery, Alabama, 1955? How did this event change the lives of African Americans? (F)
- What was Martin Luther King's dream? (F) Is it a reality today? Why or why not? (CR)
- How do you feel about the book? Would you change anything? (E)

The Greatest Muhammad Ali by Walter Dean Myers (2001). New York: Scholastic. Walter Dean Myers writes simply and elegantly about a talented, determined fighter, a nationally recognized leader of youth, and a man of strong character and moral dimension. The rich biography spans the fighter's life from his early childhood to the present day and describes how major events such as the Civil Rights Movement and the Vietnam War shaped and influenced his fascinating life.

RL: fifth grade; IL: seventh grade and up; 159 pages

Discussion and Extensions:

- What did you learn about Muhammad Ali? What were his strengths and weaknesses? (F)
- Why did Cassius Clay change his name to Muhammad Ali and how did it affect his boxing career? What major events influenced this decision (pp. 42–54)? (F)
- Compare the beliefs of Muhammad Ali and Dr. Martin Luther King Jr. How were they similar? How did they differ? How did they promote social justice? (E)
- What did the term *float like a butterfly, sting like a bee* mean? How do these words describe Muhammad Ali? Draw Ali floating like a butterfly and stinging like a bee. (FL)

- Why did Muhammad Ali refuse to be inducted into the service and how did his decision affect his boxing career? (F) What do you think about his decision? Do you think that Muhammad Ali would face the same pressures today? (CR) What would you have done? (PC)
- Compare Muhammad Ali to Joe Frazier. Include character traits and boxing style (pp. 86–91). (E)
- The author wrote: "He has always done what he believed to be the right thing. It is the most that you can ask of a life" (p. 159). What did the author mean? (I)

Writers

Authors by Request: An Inside Look at Your Favorite Writers by Janis Campbell and Cathy Collison (2002). Hillsboro, Ore.: Beyond Words Publications. Campbell and Collison, newspaper journalists, editors, and writers for young children, write about twelve favorite authors that include book lists, personal stuff, amazing facts, a short interview, and a note from students describing why they like a particular author. The authors include fascinating facts and personal information about their favorite authors, such as Patricia Polacco, who did not fully learn to read until she was fourteen (p. 65) yet went on to become a famous author and illustrator of children's books. Some of the twelve authors include Christopher Paul Curtis, J. K. Rowling, Louis Sachar, Avi, Jack Gantos, Andrew Clements, and Margaret Peterson Haddix. The authors encourage young readers to look at their website (www.beyondword.com) for the latest contests and new books. This is a good resource for teachers to share with students before introducing a particular author and book.

RL: sixth grade; IL: third through ninth grade; 118 pages

Discussion and Extensions:

- What did you learn about your favorite author and the writing process? (F)
- What questions would you like to ask him or her? (SQ)
- Write to your favorite author and use the website or author address. (EX)

- Write your opinion about why you like your favorite author and send it to the authors at the following website: www.beyond-word.com. (EX)
- Read the insert "Try This" about tips from your favorite author. Try it. Is it helpful? Would you use it again? (PC)

Bad Boy: A Memoir by Walter Dean Myers (2001). New York: Harper-Collins. This is a witty, humorous, and sensitive memoir that describes the life of this tough, talented, and ambitious writer from Harlem. Myers describes his close family life, his frequent conduct problems in school, his stuttering (and subsequent fights with peers who teased him), and his escape by reading into a world of fascinating characters, good stories, and faraway places.

> RL: sixth grade; IL: seventh grade and up; 206 pages

Discussion and Extensions:

- What challenges did Walter face in school? Why did he get in trouble? (F) Have you ever felt like him? (PC)
- Why did Walter love to read? How did reading influence his life? (F)
- What did you like most about the author? (E) What questions would you like to ask him? (SQ)
- What effects did his speech problems have on him? How did he react when he was teased? (F) What would you have done? Have you ever been part of a group that teased someone with a speech impediment or learning problem? Have you ever been teased? How did you feel? (PC)
- Look up Walter Dean Myers on the Internet. Read about his life and find out what books he has written. Read one! (R)

Calling the Doves by Juan Felipe Herrera (1995). San Francisco, Calif.: Children's Book Press. Juan Felipe Herrera describes growing up with his parents, migrant laborers in California, and the intangible gifts that he inherited from his father and mother. The narrative is written in English (with Spanish words and phrases intermingled with the text) and Span-

> RL: sixth grade; IL: all ages; 30 pages

ish. Colorful, full-page illustrations support the rich language of the prominent Mexican American poet.

Discussion and Extensions:

- The author compares the tent that he and his parents sleep in to a giant tortilla dipped in green tomato sauce (p. 6). Look at the illustration on page seven. Why did the author use this comparison? Think of another object that is like the tent and illustrate your own comparison. (DL)
- What facts did you find out about the author's life? (F) How did his parents influence his writing? (I)
- What kind of life did the young author experience as the son of migrant farm laborers? What experiences did he enjoy? What were the hardships? For example, why did the children wear paper boots made from newspaper (p. 20)? (I)
- Look on the web to find out more about living conditions, education, and rights of migrant farm laborers. Is anything being done to help migrant farm laborers and their families? (R)
- How did his father come to the United States? Why did he come? (F) Why do you think immigrants come to the United States today, some risking their lives to enter the United States? (CR) What challenges or obstacles would you face if you came to this country as a young immigrant? (PC)
- If you were interviewing the poet, what questions would you ask? (SQ)
- What is the main idea of the picture book? What do you think about the story? What do you like about the illustrations? Is there anything that you would change or more information that you would like to know? (E)

Coming Home: From the Life of Langston Hughes by Floyd Cooper (1994). New York: Putnam and Grosset Group (ALA Notable Book). Cooper uses colorful chalk illustrations and fascinating text to describe the young life of the talented poet/writer, such as his loneliness, his grandmother's stories and family heroes, and the music and rhythm that helped to shape his poignant and elegant verses.

> RL: low fourth grade; IL: third through sixth grade; 29 pages

Discussion and Extensions:

- Why did the author say that living with Grandma wasn't easy? (I)
- Who were some of the heroes "granma" told Langston about? (F)
- Why did Grandma think it was important to talk about heroes? (I)
- What is a hero? Who are your heroes? Why? (PC)
- Why does the author describe Langston as having a lonely child-hood? (I)
- Why do you think Langston liked music, church singing, and "jazzy old blues music?" (I)
- Read the poem "Hope" (p. 1). How does the poem make you feel? Have you ever experienced the feelings that Langston Hughes talks about in his short poem? (PC)
- How did you like the illustrations? What do you like about them? (E)

My Life in Dog Years by Gary Paulsen (1998). New York: Bantam Doubleday Dell Books for Young Readers, division of Random House. Gary Paulsen describes nine special dogs, each remarkable and important to the author who admits that he is a "dog person" (p. 2). He begins with Cookie, who saved his life by pulling him out of the ice, followed by Snowball, a protector and friend to the lonely seven-year-old living on an army base with his parents. Each chapter gives the reader insight into this talented writer, the challenges that he faced, and the uniqueness of each dog that lived with and loved Gary Paulsen.

RL: fifth grade; IL: fifth through ninth grade; 137 pages

Discussion and Extensions:

- Which dog do you think was the most impressive? Why? (PC)
- What did you learn about dogs? (F)
- Have you ever felt like the author, after Snowball was hit and killed by a military truck and he said that nothing would ever be right again and that he would always miss her (p. 19)? (PC)
- Write about a favorite pet. Describe how your pet looks, acts, and why he or she is so important to you. Like Paulsen's book, draw a picture to accompany your description. (PC) (EX)

- What would you like to ask the author? (SQ) Write to http://www
  .randomhouse.com/features/garypaulsen. (EX)

FANTASY

Animals

Ereth's Birthday by Avi (2000). New York: HarperTrophy. Thinking
that his good friend Poppy has forgotten his birthday, the old porcupine
trudges off to soothe his hurt feelings and to find salt, his favorite food,
near the outskirts of Dimwood Forest. Locating the hunter's cabin (and
salt), Ereth hears a cry for help and finds
Leaper, a dying fox caught in a hunter's trap. | RL: high third/low fourth
Unable to free her, Ereth promises to take care | grade; IL: third through
of her three kits (young foxes) until they can | seventh grade; 180 pages
fend for themselves. During the weeks that he is with the young foxes,
Ereth encounters Marty, the deadly fisher who plots to kill the old porcupine, fifteen dangerous hunter traps, and Bounder, the kits' arrogant
father with whom Ereth has had some history! This delightful page-
turner is the fourth in the series of tales from Dimwood Forest.

Discussion and Extensions:

- Do you think the author makes Ereth, Nimble, Tumble, Flip, and
  Marty the fisher believable? If so, in what ways? (E)
- Compare and contrast Ereth and Tumbler, the belligerent little fox.
  How are they alike? How are they different? (E)
- Do any of the author's characters remind you of anyone you know?
  If so, in what way? (PC)
- Why do you think the writer has Ereth use expressions like "holy
  horse hockey" (p. 96), "buzzard breath," "belching beavers," and
  "pink pickled pasta" (p. 4)? Make up your own alliterations (words
  that begin with the same letter sound) for Ereth. (DL)
- Read the following sentences and substitute descriptive words (i.e.,
  verb, adjective) for the words in italics: "When the porcupine broke
  away from the cabin and went *lumbering* through the snow toward
  the sound of the call, a *puzzled* Marty followed from a safe distance" (p. 44). (DL)

- Why did the author use "hammered" in the following sentence? "His heart hammered. Oh, if only he could have some!" (p. 154). Have you ever felt this way? (DL)
- Why did Ereth stay with the little foxes in the first place? (I)
- What do you like about Ereth? Is there anything you don't like about this character? Did he grow and develop in the story? If so, in what ways? (E)

Gooseberry Park by Cynthia Rylant (1995). New York: Scholastic. Stumpy, a red squirrel; Murray, a bat (both of whom live in Gooseberry Park); Kona, a Labrador retriever; and Gwendolyn, a crab (pets of Professor Albert) are all excited about Stumpy's antici-pated new family. However, after giving birth to three little squirrels, Stumpy and Murray are left homeless when a deadly ice storm strikes the old pin oak in Goose-berry Park. Leaving her babies with the little bat, Stumpy races off to get help from her old friend Kona but becomes lost when she uses the wrong address. Meanwhile, Kona rescues Murray and the baby squirrels; the three friends, Murray, Kona and Gwendolyn, devise a plan to find the lost mother squirrel.

RL: fourth grade; IL: third through seventh grade; 133 pages

Discussion and Extensions:

- Murray is nocturnal. What does "nocturnal" mean? (DL) Look on the web and find other animals that are nocturnal. (R)
- Murray told Stumpy that heart palpitations ran in his family. What does "palpitations" mean? Have you ever felt palpitations? (DL)
- Make a character web that describes Kona. Include adjectives and phrases that describe the extraordinary dog. (F) Illustrate a favorite scene or phrase that you used in your map. (EX)
- Compare Kona with Murray. How are the dog and bat similar and how are they different? (E)
- Gwendolyn tells Kona, "You try at everything you do, dear Kona. That is why I like you so" (p. 9). Who does Kona remind you of? Why? (PC)
- Gwendolyn remarks to Murray that Stumpy will be found since she can "feel it in her bones" (p. 83). What does this expression mean? Have you ever felt something "in your bones"? (DL)

- How did the author make the story believable? What realistic characteristics of bats, dogs, crabs, and squirrels did she give to Murray (a bat), Gwendolyn (a crab), Kona (a dog), and Stumpy (a squirrel)? (E)
- What questions do you have about the story? (SQ)

Poppy by Avi (1995). New York: Avon Books. Poppy, a young deer mouse, and her family have outgrown their home and wish to move to New House on the outskirts of Dimwood Forest. Mr. Ocax, the devious, great horned owl, rules the Forest and must grant permission for any travel or offenders face the consequences. Ragweed, Poppy's brash boyfriend, is eaten in the first chapter when he tries to impress Poppy and defies the cruel owl. When Poppy's father requests permission to go to New House, Mr. Ocax mysteriously refuses his request. It is up to Poppy to discover why the owl doesn't want anyone to go near New House. Along with Ereth, a grouchy old porcupine who becomes Poppy's friend and protector, the fearless mouse discovers the owl's secret and meets him in a final confrontation.

> RL: fourth grade; IL: third through eighth grade; 159 pages

Discussion and Extensions:

- Compare and contrast the two friends, Poppy and Ereth. What is similar in their personalities? What is different? (E)
- Reread Ereth's description on page 93 and draw a picture of the grumpy old porcupine. (EX)
- "She spun downstream like a whirligig" (p. 78). Why did the author use "like a whirligig"? Close your eyes and picture Poppy. What did she look like? (DL)
- "Usually the water flowed with tranquility. Not now" (p. 76). What does tranquility mean? Read the paragraph and make predictions about the meaning of the word. (P) Check your predictions in the dictionary. Use the word to describe something that you feel is tranquil. Use a color or colors to illustrate the feeling of this word. (DL)
- How did the author make Poppy, Ereth, Ragweed, and Mr. Ocax believable? What animal characteristics did they have? For example, why did Ereth not eat mice? (E)
- Which character is your favorite? Why? (E)

Tales from the House of Bunnicula by James Howe (2002). New York: Atheneum Books for Young Readers. Written from the humorous perspective of Howie Monroe (dachshund puppy and nephew of Harold Monroe, author of the first Bunnicula), the plot mysteriously resembles a Harry Potter story. Howie describes himself as an orphan and goes to the Dogwitz Academy for Canine Conjurers to conquer The-Evil-Force-Whose-Nam-C'not-Be-Spoke (really Herbert, a small kitten). Howie's editor says his book is a "terrific parody" (p. 87). Colorful characters (mostly dogs) include his beautiful golden-haired friend Delilah, Hamlet (who talks in apostrophes), the trouble-making Baco, and Happy, a toad who has been turned into a tadpole.

> RL: high fourth grade; IL: third through ninth grade; 90 pages

Discussion and Extensions:

- Howie describes himself as courageous and dauntless (p. 60). What do these words mean? Draw a picture of Howie acting courageous and dauntless (DL).
- What is the humor in the story? For example, what is humorous about Howie saying that he might even get Kibbles *and* Bits (p. 12) and enjoying his classes in Making Humans Sit, Shake, and Heel (p. 51)? (E)
- What do you think about Hamlet speaking in apostrophes? (E)
- Look up the word "conjurer." Why did the author put this work in the title? Could he have used another word? (DL)
- How do you like Howie's story? Who are your favorite characters or character? Why? (E)
- Compare Howie's story to the Harry Potter stories. How are they similar and how are they different? What are similarities or differences to other *Bunnicula* books that you have read? (E)

The Good Dog by Avi (2001). New York: Aladdin Paperbacks. McKinley, the dog of human "pup" Jack, meets Lupin, a wolf who has come out of the wilderness to find dogs to replenish her diminishing wolf pack. McKinley must decide between following Lupin and living a truly free life, or as the wolf puts it, being "a slave to humans" (p. 174). Duchess, the greyhound who runs away from her

> RL: high third/low fourth grade; IL: third through eighth grade; 243 pages

abusive owner to follow Lupin; Redburn, jealous of McKinley's leadership and anxious to follow his master's orders to track down Duchess; and Aspen, McKinley's affectionate, faithful friend, are believable characters in Avi's story about freedom, loyalty, power, and love. The story is told from the perspective of McKinley, a malamute and head dog of the dogs from Steamboat Springs.

Discussion and Extensions:

- What do you think about the story? Rate the book on a scale of 1 to 3 (1 being the highest). What did you like the most? What did you like the least? (E)
- What did you learn about the behavior of dogs? For example, how did McKinley show submission to Lupin (p. 56) or affection to Aspen (p. 118–19)? (F)
- Compare McKinley and Lupin. How are the dog and wolf alike? How are they different? (E)
- Reread pages 118 and 174. Why did McKinley submit to Lupin and then try to save her life? (I)
- Avi describes the snow as light, "like summer dust" (p. 199). What did the author mean? What else could snow be like? (DL)
- What is a glowbox (p. 217)? What is a small buzz box (p. 220)? Why did the author choose these descriptions? Select common household items (e.g., oven, computer) and use your own descriptors to identify these items in "dog language." (DL)
- What did you think about the story? Is it believable? Why did the author write the story from McKinley's perspective? (E)
- Lupin's powerful and distinctive howl in the beginning of the story (chapter 7, p. 56) is identical to McKinley's howl that "vaulted as high as the sky" at the end of the story (chapter 30, p. 238). Why do you think the author described both animals in the same way? (I)

The Grand Escape by Phyllis Reynolds Naylor (1993). New York: Bantam Doubleday Dell. Marco and Polo, well cared for and loved house cats, are bored and plot to escape to the outdoors. Once out, they encounter other cats such as the friendly calico cat Carlotta, Elvis (a singing cat), and Texas Jake (TJ), the big, rough leader who requires that they find the

RL: 4.2; IL: third through eighth grade; 147 pages

answer to three mysteries in order to sleep in the communal loft. Surviving river rats, Bertram the Bad dog, and a moving vehicle are all part of the dangers that await them as they solve each of TJ's mysteries.

Discussion and Extensions:

- Why do the young cats want to escape to the outdoors? (I) What about freedom is so important when you don't have it? (CR)
- The author describes the "steamy white heat of summer" (p. 1). How does her description make you feel? Draw a picture that illustrates steamy white heat. (DL)
- Of all of the cats (Marco, Polo, Carlotta, Texas Jake, and Elvis), which character do you like best? Why? (E) Do any of them remind you of humans you know? (PC)
- How does the author add humor to the story? For example, what is humorous about the mystery and solution to why humans have no hair covering? What makes it rain? (pp. 52, 53). (E)
- When Boots sees Marco and Polo, he tells the other cats that they shouldn't take in just any stray cat that Carlotta brings in. "Can't we get members of a higher caliber than this?" (p.53). What did Boots mean when he said "caliber?" Make a word map that describes "caliber." Include several examples, synonyms, and your own sentence. Draw a picture of a cat of high caliber. Who do you know that is of high caliber? Use the dictionary as a resource. (DL)
- How did the cats solve TJ's three mysteries? What was the mystery inside Bertram the Bad's doghouse? Where did the water go after it rained? Finally, where did Mr. Murphy go when he got into his car? (F)
- How did you like the story? What did you think about the ending? How did the author resolve the issue of freedom with the two cats? (E)

Ghosts

Pleasing the Ghost by Sharon Creech (1996). New York: HarperTrophy. Nine-year-old Dennis is haunted by ghosts but not by the one he really wants—his father. Dennis's father died over a year ago but so far he has only been visited by his Great Gran, his old cat Choo, an old man who used to live next door, and a few others. Now a whistling wind and blue smoke has brought Uncle Arvie (who died of a stroke that causes him to speak in two- and three-syllable nonsense words) with three wishes for Dennis to fulfill: find a hidden letter, finish an anniver-

> RL: second grade; IL: third through fifth grade; short chapters; 89 pages

sary painting, and dig up Aunt Julia's favorite rose bush! Creech writes a human story with heavenly overtones of caring and hopefulness.

Discussion and Extensions:

- The author describes Uncle Arvie's hug like "tickling cobwebs" (p. 7). Have you ever felt a hug like this? Describe a hug from someone using your own words. Start with "My (mother's, father's, sister's, grandma's, grandpa's) hug felt like _____." (DL)
- How many syllables are in the following words that Uncle Arvie uses to convey his thoughts? Pailandplop, foodle, doodle, creppit, Heartfoot? What does "Pin Heartfoot" mean? Use context clues (p. 62). Make up a three-syllable word for Uncle Arvie. (DL)
- Why is Uncle Arvie the ghost that haunts Dennis? (I)
- Why did Billy see Uncle Arvie when he was invisible to everyone else except Dennis? (I)
- Write another chapter. What ghost, if any, visits Dennis? (EX)
- What do you think about the story? Is it believable? What do you think about the characters? Did Dennis change from the beginning of the story? (E)

Something Upstairs by Avi (1988). New York: Avon Books. Kenny Huldorf reluctantly follows his parents to their new home in Providence, Rhode Island, that was once owned by Daniel Stillwell in 1789. When exploring, Kenny hears scratching sounds in the attic and discovers Caleb, a ghost who was once a slave in 1789 and murdered by an unknown assailant. Caleb wants Kenny to return with him to 1789 to help him find his murderer. Once back in the past, Kenny dis-

> RL: middle fourth grade; IL: third through eighth grade; 119 pages

covers that he, too, will become a spirit, trapped in the eighteenth century, if he does not fulfill the demands of evil Mr. Willinghast.

Discussion and Extensions:

- Why was Caleb trapped in Kenny's attic? (F)
- Why was Kenny likely to be trapped in the past? (F)
- Who was Pardon Willinghast? In what era was he "alive"? Who were his friends, Ormsbee and Seagrave? (F)
- According to the author, the murder of a slave was not considered important in 1789. Why? (I)
- Was the story believable? Did you feel like you were in a different century? Would you have changed anything? (E)
- Why did the author select the late 1700s for the murder to occur? Could he have written his story in the present century? Could a similar event happen today? (CR)

The Doll in the Garden by Mary Downing Hahn (1989). New York: Avon Books. Ten-year-old Ashley and her mother have just moved to an apartment room in an old house owned by the grumpy, eighty-eight-year-old Miss Cooper. Told to keep out of the forbidden garden, Ashley and her neighbor Kristi follow a mysterious white cat into the garden and discover an antique doll and mysterious note of apology from "Carrie" to "Louisa." A garden hedge that separates the past from the present, a sick little girl suffering from consumption, and two neighbor girls who become ghosts when they follow the white cat, Snowball, are all part of this fascinating ghost story.

> RL: middle fourth grade; IL: third through seventh grade; 20 chapters, 128 pages

Discussion and Extensions:

- The author describes the snapping sound of Miss Cooper's fingers like "sandpaper being rubbed together" (p. 22). Why did she use this comparison? What does it make you think of? (DL)
- "Her face was furrowed with wrinkles, and her nose jutted out like a hawk's beak, sharp and cruel" (p. 1). Draw a picture of Miss Cooper that matches this description. What other words can you think of that mean the same thing as "furrowed" and "jutted out?" (DL)
- How do you know that Snowball is a ghost? What clues does the author provide? (F)

- Who were the ghosts in this story? How many ghosts were in the story? How do you know? (F)
- Draw a character web that describes Miss Cooper. Include physical characteristics and behavior. Include information about "Carrie," the young Miss Cooper. (F)
- How did Louisa change Miss Cooper? Ashley? Kristi? (I)
- Why do you think the author changed Miss Cooper back into a young girl when she crossed the hedge with Kristi and Ashley? How did this affect the story? (I)
- What is consumption? How did this disease affect individuals in the 1800s? (F)
- What did you think about the story? Would you recommend it to a friend? Why or why not? (E)

The Heavenly Village by Cynthia Rylant (1999). New York: Scholastic. This sensitive short story is about seven angels who are waylaid on their way to Perfect Happiness—Heaven. Each character (a reluctant spirit) has not finished his or her story, thus God has placed them in a special stopping place called the Heavenly Village, to sort out a few things before they go to Heaven. Through simple text, the author describes characters like Everett, who wants a second chance to find beauty; Violet Rose, a lovely young woman who must wait for her cats; and Dr. Blake, who wants more memories of his baby son, Jay.

> RL: fifth grade;
> IL: fourth
> through seventh
> grade; 95 pages

Discussion and Extensions:

- What character did you like the best? Why? (E)
- Did the characters Evertt, Violet Rose, Harold, Cordie, and Thomas grow and develop in the author's story? If so, in what way? (E)
- Select your favorite character and finish his or her story. Write about Evertt, the timekeeper; Violet Rose, the baker; Harold and his dog, Fortune; Isham, the magician; Raphael Blake, the doctor; Cordie, the runner; or Thomas, the potter. (EX)
- Write a letter from Isham the magician to Violet Rose, the one that he wants to write but so far, has not been able to do (p. 64). (EX)
- The elderly woman in the gardener's smock tells Everett, "No one dies. They just relocate "(p. 20). What did she mean? (I)

- If you were going to spend time in the Heavenly Village, what would you want to do? What is the value of such a place? (PC)(CR)
- How did you feel about the book? What did you like about it? What would you change? (E)

Fairy Tales

Just Ella by Margaret Peterson Haddix (1999). New York: Simon and Schuster. In this Cinderella story, Ella discovers that her Prince Charming is not what she expected. Although Prince Charming is handsome, he is shallow, selfish, and only interested in himself. When Ella tries to break the engagement, she is imprisoned in the dungeon until Mary, a servant girl, comes to her aid. Colorful characters include the evil Madame Bisset; Jed, Lord Reston's sensitive, intelligent son; and the Step-Evils, Ella's stepsisters, Corimunde and Griselda.

RL: fifth grade; IL: sixth grade and up; 185 pages

Discussion and Extensions:

- Why did Ella call the prince an insensitive dullard and callous monster? How is he different than the European fairy tale character? Is he a believable character? If so, in what ways? (Reread p. 139) (E)
- Is Ella a believable character? Did she grow and develop throughout the story? (E)
- Compare and contrast Prince Charming and Jed Reston. How are they alike and how are they different? (E)
- "'Let go of me,' I said, ice dripping from every word" (p. 105). What did Ella mean when she said her voice was like ice? How does ice feel? To what other emotion can you compare ice? (DL)
- Do you think Ella believes in godmothers? Why? Use facts from the story to support your answer. (I)
- Write an epilogue from Mary's perspective. What happened to her? (EX)
- Compare *Just Ella* to the European fairy tale. Is Ella like Cinderella? What is the theme or main idea in both stories? How are they alike or different? Draw a Venn diagram comparing and contrasting both stories. (E)

The Frog Prince Continued by Jon Scieszka (1991). New York: Viking.
Beginning where the traditional fairy tale "Frog Prince" ended, the
prince and princess are not happily married ever after.
The princess has grown tired of her frog prince sticking out his tongue, spending time in the pond, and
hopping on the furniture. The prince escapes to the
forest to find the witch who could turn him back into

> RL: low third
> grade; IL: all
> ages; 27 pages
> (picture book)

a frog. Scieszka's ending has a surprise twist that leaves the prince and
princess living happily ever after. Steve Johnson's humorous paintings
of spooky witches, dark forests, and slimy frogs fit perfectly with
Scieszka's zany text.

Discussion and Extensions:

- Why are the princess and the prince unhappy? Who is at fault?
  Why? (I)
- The prince encounters three witches but all have different plans for
  him. Who are witches? (F) How does the author tie in other fairy
  tales? (I)
- Read the European fairy tale. How was the prince changed in
  Scieszka's version? How is the princess different in the two ver-
  sions? Is the theme or main idea the same? (E)
- What did you think about the story? Rate it on a scale of 1 to 3
  (1 being the highest). Would you have changed anything? (E)
- Write the story from the princesses' point of view. Change the ending. Illustrate your story. (EX)

The Three Little Wolves and the Big Bad Pig by Eugene
Trivizas (1993). New York: Macmillan. Rather than
three little pigs, the author depicts three gentle wolves
that are stalked by a big bad pig. After failing to keep
the pig away with houses built of brick, concrete, and

> RL: third
> grade; IL: third
> through ninth
> grade; 29 pages

armor plates and metal padlocks, they win the pig's heart with a house
made of flowers!

Discussion and Extensions:

- Write the story from the perspective of the big bad pig. Why is he
  so big and bad? (EX)

- Compare this story with the European fairy tale. What are the similarities and differences in characters, events, and theme? Which one do you prefer? Why? (E)
- Where is the humor in the tale? Why did the author select flowers to resolve the conflict? (E)
- The wolves were finally successful with their fourth attempt at problem solving. How many times was the pig successful in blowing down their houses? Represent this amount in a fraction; in a decimal. Illustrate this problem. (EX)
- What is the theme or main idea of the story? Is the theme important? (E) Can you relate the theme and characters to events that occur today? Who does the big bad pig make you think of? The little wolves? (CR)

The Three Pigs by David Wiesner (2001) (Caldecott Medal). New York: Clarion Books, Houghton Mifflin. Wiesner's surreal story literally jumps off the page as the three pigs are blown out of the story to meet other fairy tale characters. Cartoon captions and surrealistic paintings show pigs flying through the air to meet the cat and the fiddle, rescue the dragon as it is | RL: low third grade; IL: all ages; 37 pages |
about to be slain by the prince, and reenter the story in time to outwit the hungry, tenacious wolf. Many pages have little or no text.

Discussion and Extensions:

- Write an epilogue to this fairy tale with cartoon captions. Did they all live happily ever after? What happened to the wolf? (EX)
- Rewrite the story from the wolf's perspective or the cat and the fiddle. (EX)
- Look at the illustrations. Why do you think the artist received the Caldecott Medal for his outstanding illustrations? What do you like about them? Does anything bother you? (E)
- Compare the story to the original "Three Little Pigs." How did the author change the story events? Who was the villain in both versions? Was the theme the same? (E)
- Write a short review for another reader. Include what you think are the strengths and weaknesses of the picture book. (E)
- What questions do you have about the story? (SQ)

The True Story of the 3 Little Pigs by Jon Scieszka (1989). New York: Viking. Written by A. Wolf, this tale is about the wolf being framed for a crime that he did not do, or didn't mean to do! As the wolf notes, it was all on account of needing a cup of sugar and having a cold! This clever story is told from the wolf's perspective and offers insight into how stories change by taking another point of view!

> RL: second grade; IL: second through ninth grade; 28 pages (picture book)

Discussion and Extensions:

- What do you like about the wolf? Is he a believable fantasy character? (E) Have you ever felt like him, blamed for something you did not do? (PC)
- Compare this version with the European version. How did the author change the story events and theme? Why do you think he took the side of the wolf? (E)
- Write your own story from the perspective of the first little pig. Change events and make up your own ending. (EX)
- What does the author mean when he says "dead as a doornail" (p. 19)? Use this expression in your own story. (DL)
- Look at the illustrations. What is humorous about them? (E) What information does the artist portray that is not included in the author's story? (I)
- Out of the three little pigs, how many little pigs ended up as hamburger? Represent this number in a fraction and in a decimal. Illustrate the fraction and decimal. (EX)

Identity/Solving Problems

REM World by Rodman Philbrick (2000). New York: Scholastic. Arthur Wordbury, called Biscuit Butt by jeering peers, wants to lose weight. He orders a weight program through a comic book called "REM World" that guarantees losing weight while sleeping. The problems begin when Arthur fails to read all of the directions in the REM World package and falls asleep in the basement. Unknowingly, the sleeping teenager puts the universe—and himself—into a spiral that

> RL: fifth grade; IL: fourth–eighth grades; 190 pages

is headed for oblivion. Waking up to find his "other self" in REM World, Arthur meets the Frog People, the giant Grog and his lost fiancée Droll, a fury companion named Morf, the demon Vydel, and the Cloud People who give him a new name, Arthur Courage. When "Nothingness" begins to invade the empty spaces of his basement (as his unconscious self is fast asleep), it is up to Arthur Courage to save the universe and himself.

Discussion and Extensions:

- Do you think the author made REM World believable? Why or why not? (E)
- What do you think about Arthur? Is he a believable character? Do you like him? Did he grow and develop? (E)
- Arthur was teased because of his weight. Have you ever been part of a group that made fun of others? Have you ever been teased? What does it feel like? (PC) Why do you think people make fun of others? (CR)
- Read the description of the demon's box (p. 171) and illustrate what you think it looks like. (EX)
- Why did the Cloud People select the name Arthur Courage? (I)
- How did Arthur live up to his new name? (I)
- How does this book compare to another fantasy that you have read? Draw a Venn Diagram with similarities in the overlapping sections and differences in the separate parts. Which book do you prefer? Why? (E)
- Predict what will happen to Morph, Leela, and Vydel (P). Write an epilogue that tells their story. (EX)

Maniac Magee by Jerry Spinelli (1990). Boston: Little Brown. Jeffery "Maniac" Magee is an orphan. Unable to live with his unhappy, arguing aunt and uncle, Jeffery runs away to begin the legendary feats that make him a household name in the segregated neighborhoods of the East and West End. Bookish Amanda Beale and "bad" Mars Bars Thompson from the East End; old Earl Grayson, the grizzly park attendant; and rough John McNab and his unruly younger brothers from the

| RL: fourth grade;
IL: fourth–ninth
grades; 184 pages |

West End play pivotal roles in a story that crosses race boundaries, endures power struggles, and builds relationships in the most unlikely of places.

Discussion and Extensions:

- When Amanda throws her book at Maniac, the book comes "flap-ping like a wounded duck" and falls at Jeffery's feet. Why did the author use this comparison? Draw a picture that illustrates this im-age (p. 13). (DL)
- When young Arnold Jones is thrown into Finsterald's back yard by some high school kids, Arnold's teeth are "chattering like snare drums" (p. 18). What does the author want you to think of? What other comparison could you use? (DL)
- When Jeffery leaves Hollidaysburg, it takes him one year to get to Two Mills, a 200 mile journey (p. 8). "Sure, two hundred miles is a long way, especially on foot, but the year that it took him to cover it was about fifty-one weeks more than he needed—figuring the way he could run, even then" (p. 8). If the 200-mile journey took Jeffery fifty-one weeks, about how many miles did he run in a day? (EX)
- Compare and contrast Maniac to Mars Bar. How are they alike and how are they different? (E)
- Do you think the author represented all perspectives in his story? Did he avoid stereotypes? Were any perspectives left out or under-represented? (E)
- Why did Earl Grayson never learn to read? How did Maniac teach Earl to read? (F)
- When Grayson reads his first sentence, "His smile was so wide he'd have had to break it into sections to fit it through a doorway" (102). What did the author mean? (DL)
- Have you ever felt like Earl Grayson when you did something that you thought was impossible? (PC) Write about or illustrate the sit-uation. (EX)
- What events make this novel a fantasy? What events could only happen in your imagination? What makes the story believable? (E)

Stargirl by Jerry Spinelli (2000). New York: Knopf. Stargirl Caraway, a tenth grader, is a new girl at Mica, Arizona, High School. She is differ-ent from the others—kind and generous, and wears bizarre clothes and no make-up. At first, Stargirl is accepted because of her individuality.

Then the newness wears off when she continues her strange behaviors, such as cheering for an opposing team. Classmates decide to shun her; they ignore her and refuse to talk to her. Leo Borlock, drawn to Stargirl because of her uniqueness, must choose between protecting his own popularity (ignoring Stargirl as well) or remaining faithful to a close friend. His choice brings consequences and an unexpected climax when Stargirl demonstrates how self-worth, individualism, and bravery can strip away the ugly shallowness of group behavior.

RL: fourth grade; IL: junior high and above; 183 pages

Discussion and Extensions:

- The author uses the idiom "like a deer caught in headlights" to describe Stargirl's large eyes: "She wore no makeup, and her eyes were the biggest I had ever seen, like deer's eyes caught in headlights" (p. 5). What does this mean? Describe someone you know that has eyes like deer's eyes caught in headlights. (DL)
- Leo thinks Stargirl has "chocolaty eyelashes" (p. 39). What does this mean? Think of two other adjectives that you could use to describe Stargirl's eyes. (DL)
- When Stargirl brags about winning the state speech contest, Leo tells Stargirl that she is "counting her chickens before they hatch" (p. 147). What does this idiom mean? Have you ever counted your chickens before they hatched? Why is this a dangerous thing to do? (DL)
- The story starts out with Leo receiving a mysterious porcupine tie for his birthday and ends fifteen years later with the same event. Why did the author do this? What do you think he is trying to tell the reader? (I)
- Leo chose to value the opinions of peers rather than Stargirl. Why? (I) What would you have done in his situation? (PC)
- In what way did Leo betray Susan (Stargirl)? In what way did Susan betray herself? (chapter 26). Use story information to support your answer. (I)
- Archie said, "Star people are rare. You'll be lucky to meet another"(p. 177). What did he mean? (I)
- What is the message or theme of the story? Do you think it is important? In what ways? (E)

Things Not Seen by Andrew Clements (2002). New York: Penguin Putnam. Fifteen-year-old Bobby Philips wakes up to find that he is invisible. Only his parents and newfound friend Alicia, a blind girl whom he met at the library, know his secret. Alicia cannot keep the secret from her parents and both teenagers and fathers, scientists by training, try

> RL: fifth grade; IL: sixth grade and up; 251 pages

to unravel and reverse the strange and dangerous phenomenon. This is a suspenseful story about friendship, identity, and the dangers of being outside the norm.

Discussion and Extensions:

- Bobby describes his neighbor, Mrs. Trent, as pulling the "old get your foot in the door with some cookies trick" (64). What did he mean? (DL) Do you know anyone like Mrs. Trent? (PC)
- Bobby describes his fear like this: "It's up past terror, past panic. I'm thinking this must be dread. Except I'm not thinking" (p. 58). Have you ever felt invisible, afraid, or alone? (PC) Use colors and shapes to illustrate this feeling or write a short paragraph about a time when you have felt like Bobby. (EX)
- Why did Bobby and Alicia become such good friends? (I)
- Did you like the story? Were the characters believable? In what ways did Bobby grow and develop? Would you recommend the book to another reader? (E)
- Predict what happened to Bobby, to Alicia. (P) Write an epilogue that takes place ten years after the story ended. (EX)

Mystery

Gathering Blue by Lois Lowry (2000). New York: Random House. Kira, who is lame, is a gifted weaver. When her mother dies, she is chosen by the powerful Council of Guardians to become the next Robe-Threader. Kira is to design a symbolic Robe worn by the prestigious Singer for his performance at the annual "Gathering" when he sings about the community's destruction (the Ruin), rebirth, and

> RL: fifth grade; IL: fifth–ninth grades; 215 pages

future. Soon, Kira and her new friend, Thomas, also an orphan chosen by the Council for his talents in woodcarving, discover that secrets, mystery, and danger surround their privileged lives in the Council Edifice. A companion book to *The Giver*, *Gathering Blue* addresses similar issues of freedom, choice, and survival.

Discussion and Extensions:

- Why do you think the author created the main character with a lame leg? How did Kira's physical disability affect the story? (I)
- Why was Kira's scrap of cloth and Matt's piece of wood so important to them? (I)
- "At night, before she slept, Kira held the scrap of cloth that had so often *assuaged* her fears and even answered her questions" (p. 167). Predict the meaning of "assuaged" from the context. Look it up in the dictionary. Read the sentence and provide another word that would make sense in the sentence. Use the word in a sentence to describe someone or something that has assuaged your fears. (DL)
- What freedoms did the Council take away from Jo, Matt, and Kira? (F) Why did Kira wish that she could leave her new comfortable life and return to the life she had known (p. 154)? (I)
- Compare Kira's community to the United States. What freedoms do we have that Kira did not have in her community? Do you see similarities to Kira's world and our present-day world? (E)
- "Looking down at the *sea of faces*, Kira gradually recognized people here and there" (p. 175). What did the author mean by "sea of faces?" Describe an event where you were in a "sea of faces." (DL)
- What do you think about the story? The setting? The characters? Are they believable? (E)
- Predict what happened to Kira, Thomas, and Jo after the story ended. (P) For example, did the children stay in the community and rebuild a better life or did they escape to the village of the healing? Was Kira ever reunited with her father? Write an epilogue. (EX)

Holes by Louis Sachar (1998) (Newbery Award, National Book Award). New York: Farrar, Straus and Giroux. Stanley Yelnats IV, an overweight middle school student teased by peers, is sent to Camp Green Lake for a crime that he did not commit. Bad luck runs in his family after his

great-great-grandfather failed to honor a promise and
received a curse on himself and future generations of
Yelnats. While digging holes at Camp Green Lake,
Stanley finds a good friend (Zero), encounters dangerous enemies (the Warden, Mr. Sir), and discovers secrets about the dangerous outlaw Kissing Kate Barlow
and his great-great-grandfather, the first Stanley Yelnats.

> RL: high
> third/low fourth
> grades; IL: fifth
> grade and up;
> 232 pages with
> short characters

Discussion and Extensions:

- How did Stanley's great-great-grandfather begin the curse that followed the Yelnats family? (F)
- Reread the description of the Warden (p. 66) and draw a picture of
  this crafty character. (EX) How do you think she acquired the black
  turquoise-studded boots? (Clues are on p. 122). (I)
- Why did Zero refuse to answer questions in Camp Green Lake? (I)
- What would you have done if you were Zero? (PC)
- Stanley and Zero eat onions to survive in the desert. One day, Stanley asks his friend how many onions they would have eaten if they'd
  been gone a week and each had eaten twenty onions a day. Zero responds, "Two hundred and eighty onions" (p. 186). Is Zero correct?
  How did Zero come up with this sum? Describe the steps you followed to support or refute Zero's answer. (EX)
- Develop a math problem about a particular event in the book (e.g.,
  how many holes did Stanley dig in X number of days?). (EX)
- What do you think about the story? Is Stanley a believable character? Does he grow and develop? What did he mean when he said,
  "He liked himself now" (p. 186)? Would you recommend the story
  to another reader? Why or why not? (E)
- Select a color (or colors) and draw lines, symbols, or objects that
  represent the main idea or theme. Illustrate your favorite part.
  (EX)

The Hostile Hospital: A Series of Unfortunate Events by Lemony Snicket
(2001). New York: HarperCollins. In this story, one
of a series, the unfortunate Baudelaire orphans are
trying to escape capture after being framed for the
murder of Count Olaf—who really murdered

> RL: sixth grade; IL:
> fourth through ninth
> grades; 255 pages

Jacques Snicket! They hide in the Heimlich Hospital where they volunteer as VFD (volunteers fighting disease) to try to find lost files revealing who really escaped the fire in which their parents were presumed dead! When the evil Count captures Violet and attempts to give her a cranioectomy (a procedure that removes the head!), it is up to Klaus and Sunny to rescue their sister and obtain the valuable files. But, characteristically, the author ends the story with the orphans in another predicament!

Discussion and Extensions:

• What is the problem that Violet, Klaus, and Sunny face this time? What is Count Olaf's plan to obtain the Baudelaire fortune? (F)
• Read the description of the "villainous Esmé Squalor (p. 115) and draw a picture of Count Olaf's evil girlfriend. (EX)
• What does the author mean by the expression "a slave to fashion" (p. 115). Do you know anyone like this? (DL)
• What does the author mean when he said that Klaus and Sunny "felt the unpleasant fluttering of butterflies in their stomach" (p. 172)? Write about a time when you have felt this way. What other words can you use to describe this feeling? (DL)
• The author uses the word "spurious" in the following sentence: "Their disguises looked spurious—a word which here means nothing at all like a real doctor" (p. 164). He also uses it when he talks about "spurious doctors" (p. 216) and a "spurious intercom" (p. 239). What does this word mean? Use this word to describe something that you have experienced. (DL)
• How did the author use humor in this book? What did you find humorous? (E)
• Compare this book to another book by Lemony Snicket. Which story/plot did you prefer? Why? (E)
• What do you think happens to Violet, Klaus, and Sunny in the trunk of Count Olaf's car? Where are the precious files and what secrets do they reveal? (P) Write another short chapter about the children. Use the phrase "butterflies in their stomach" and the word "spurious." (EX)

The Miserable Mill: A Series of Unfortunate Events by Lemony Snicket (2000). New York: HarperCollins. Wit and humor describe this dark, gloomy tale (book 4 in the series) about the three Baudelaire orphans' "unfortunate" experiences at the Lucky Smells Lumbermill. Once again, fourteen-year-old Violet, twelve-year-old Klaus, and baby Sunny find themselves in the hands of evil Count Olaf and his

> RL: sixth grade; IL: fourth–ninth grades; 194 pages

scheme to obtain their family fortune. Rich vocabulary, figurative language, a fast-moving plot, and colorful characters provide for another suspenseful and fun read.

Discussion and Extensions:

- What clues does the author provide that alerts readers to Count Olaf's presence at the Lucky Smells Lumbermill? (I)
- Reread the author's description of Foreman Flacutono and his curly white wig and blinking, dark beady eyes (p. 33). Close your eyes and imagine the picture in your head. With crayons, pencil, or pastels, draw your image of Foreman Flacutono. (EX)
- What does the author mean when he writes, "Let's not split hairs" (p. 156) or "Gum up the works" (p. 170). Write about a time when you have gummed up the works or split hairs doing something. Illustrate the literal meanings of the phrases. (DL)
- According to author Lemony Snicket, what does "quiet as mice" mean and why *doesn't* this describe how Violet and Sunny tiptoed across the dormitory and walked out into the night? Why does the author prefer "quiet as mimes?" (Reread p. 81.) (DL)
- How does the author use humor in his story? What is funny? (E)
- Compare this story to another story in the series. Which story do you prefer? What characters do you like? Why? (E)
- Predict what else could have happened after the accident in the lumber mill. (P) Change the ending and write an epilogue about what happens to Violet, Klaus, Sunny, and Count Olaf. (EX)

The Reptile Room: A Series of Unfortunate Events by Lemony Snicket (1999). New York: HarperCollins. This is the second book about the three orphaned Baudelaire children: Violet, age fourteen; Klaus, age twelve; and baby Sunny. After escaping from their evil, distant relative Count Olaf who only wants their inheritance (book 1), the three children are put in

> RL: sixth grade; IL: fourth–ninth grades; 190 pages

the care of another distant relative, Dr. Montgomery. "Uncle Monty" is a kind soul and a herpetologist—an expert in snakes. When Uncle Monty's new research assistant arrives, the children recognize a disguised Count Olaf and realize all of their lives are in danger again!

Discussion and Extensions:

- Why do you think the author kills Uncle Monty in chapter 6? (I) If you were the author, what would you have done? (PC)
- Draw a picture of Stephano, i.e., Count Olaf. (Reread chapter 4.) (EX)
- In this fantasy, what events are impossible in this story? How does the author make the story believable? (E)
- Which of the Baudelaire twins do you relate to, like, or know someone like? (PC)
- What does "feeling like a fifth wheel" mean (p. 113)? When have you felt like a fifth wheel? Illustrate this phrase. (DL)
- Who is Dr. Lucafont? (F) What clues can you find that make you mistrust this person? (I)
- What clues did Violet find in Stephano's suitcase? (F) How did this information expose the murderer (p. 162)? (I)

Time Travel/Outer Space

Company's Coming by Arthur Yorinks (1988). New York: Hyperion Books for Children. This is a clever picture book with cartoon-like illustrations by David Small (Caldecott Honor Medal) about getting to know and appreciate others different from ourselves (in this instance, spacemen!). Illustrations that picture look-alike homes and a spaceship circling overhead introduce the humorous and insightful story about Shirley and Moe from Bellmore who invite guests to dinner and find two additional visitors from outer space on their doorstep. A frightened Moe calls in the FBI, Pentagon, Army, Air Force, and Marines to confront the gentle, gift-bearing aliens.

RL: second grade; IL: second through fourth grade; 26 pages

Discussion and Extensions:

- How would you feel if two spacemen knocked on your front door? What would you do? Would you react like Moe or Shirley? Why? (PC)

- Why did the illustrator show look-alike houses on the front cover? What does this have to do with the story? (I)
- What do you think about the story? Would you have changed anything? What do you think about the illustrations? What do you like about them? How do they help tell the story? (E)
- How are Shirley and Moe alike? How are they different? (E) Do you know any people like them? In what way? (PC)
- Do Shirley and Moe change or develop over the course of the story? (E)
- What is the theme or main idea of the story? Do you think it is important? (E)
- Write a sequel to the story and compare it to the author's sequel, *Company's Going.* (EX)

Company's Going by Arthur Yorinks (2001). New York: Hyperion Books for Children. In this sequel to *Company's Coming,* Shirley and Moe are invited to travel with the two spacemen to their new planet to cater a wedding reception featuring Shirley's famous meatballs. When the humans arrive, they receive the same hysterical greetings that their

> RL: second grade; IL: through fourth grade; 26 pages

spacemen received on Earth, except this time Moe gets hit by a nervous uncle and his ray gun! David Small's illustrations continue to delight and add humor to this clever sequel.

Discussion and Extensions:

- What is the message (theme) the author expresses in *Company's Going*? What do you think about the setting? Does it support the story/theme? (E)
- Compare Shirley and Moe. How are they the same? How do they differ? (E) Do they change from the way they were depicted in *Company's Coming*? (E)
- What customs are similar on the planet Nextoo and in Bellmore? (E)
- What information is in the illustrations and is not in the text? (I)
- Which story (*Company's Coming; Company's Going*) did you prefer? Why? (E)

Hey Kid, Want to Buy a Bridge? The Time Warp Trio by Jon Scieszka (2002). New York: Penguin Group. Joe, Sam, and Fred think they are going into the future to steal an invention and see their granddaughters but instead are catapulted a hundred years into the past. There they meet their granddaughters (who are as surprised as they are to be there), a depressed Thomas Edison, and a frustrated Washington Roebling—builder of the Brooklyn Bridge. Fact and fiction are intertwined in this zany story about making things right before they go too wrong!

> RL: second grade; IL: second–sixth grades; 74 pages

Discussion and Extensions:

- The Time Warp Trio has already visited the future. Predict what will happen to you in one hundred years. (P) Write about (or illustrate) your trip to the future and describe what you will find. (EX)
- What facts did you learn in this story? (F)
- Use the Internet and find out all you can about Thomas Edison and Washington Roebling. Did the author base his descriptions about Edison and Roebling on any facts? (R)
- What did you think about the story? What did you like? Would you change anything? (E)
- Read another *Time Warp Trio* book and compare characters, theme, and plot. How are they alike and how are they different? Which one did you prefer? Why? (E)

Running Out of Time by Margaret Peterson Haddix (1997). New York: Simon and Schuster. It is 1870 in the frontier village of Clifton, Indiana, where Jessie lives with her family. When a diphtheria epidemic threatens the life of Jessie's sister and others in Clifton, Jessie is told by her frightened mother that Clifton is really a historically preserved village, made up of twenty-five volunteer families who wanted to escape the complex life of the twentieth century, and one that tourists can view from the outside world of 1996. However, rules have changed since the inception of the village; no one can leave Clifton, and the authorities will only use medicine that is available in the 1870s.

> RL: fourth grade; IL: third–eighth grades; 184 pages

Jessie's task is to escape into the outside world, find Mr. Neely, a link to the project, and return with medicine. Jessie finds a foreign world (e.g., telephones, cars, television) and an enemy, rather than a friend, who wants her silenced. This is a fast-paced story with lots of surprises!

Discussion and Extensions:

- Why did Ma send Jessie rather than trying to escape herself? (I)
- What is a "daguerreotype"? Reread the paragraph on top of page 55 for context clues. Make a prediction, then check your prediction with the dictionary. Visit a historical museum and find examples of daguerreotypes. (DL)
- What does the expression mean, "You bite off more than you can chew?" Reread page 142, third paragraph, to find more clues. When have you felt that you have bitten off more than you could chew? Illustrate this expression. (DL)
- Why did Clifton become so dangerous? (I)
- Why do you think that the author wrote the story? What was the theme or themes? Is the theme meaningful today? (E)
- Predict what life will be fifty years from now. What will you be able to do that you can't do now? (P) How old will you be? Draw a picture of yourself in the future. Write about what you will be doing. (EX) Rate the story from 1 to 3, with 1 being the highest. What did you like about the story? Would you have changed anything? (E)

Sam Samurai: The Time Warp Trio by Jon Scieszka (2001). New York: Penguin Group. Joe, Sam, and Fred, spirited away to 1600 Japan by Uncle Joe's magic "Book," encounter Honda, a samurai warrior; Tokugawa, the powerful shogun; and Owattabutt, his ruthless leader of the Red Devils. Learning about Japanese customs, finding ways out of near fatal events, and being rescued by their great-great-grandchildren are all part of this humorous chapter book.

RL: second grade; IL: second–sixth grades; 85 pages

Discussion and Extensions:

- Joe said that they were too "freaked out" to move (p. 18). What does this expression mean? When have you ever felt freaked out? (DL)

- The red-armored samurai had a scar that "made his lip curl into a nasty sneer" (p. 54). What does sneer mean? Read the next sentence and substitute an adjective that describes a sneer. Draw the samurai with the "sneer" on his face. (DL)
- Joe couldn't come up with entertainment to satisfy the gatekeeper. He said that it was like a horrible school nightmare like when you show up for math class in your underwear and find out that there is a math test (p. 52). What is your school nightmare? (PC) Illustrate your nightmare or Joe's school nightmare. (EX)
- What did you learn about 1600 Japan? The customs (p. 38), dress (pp. 24, 69), food (p. 68), and poetry? (F) Look on the web and compare present-day customs in Japan to those described in *Sam Samurai*. What are the same and what are different? (E)
- When the boys didn't have a passport, Sam said, "Oh, now we are toast" (p. 46). What does this expression mean? When were you *toast*? (DL)
- The boys said that they sliced off a samurai's head 500 years before they were born. If they are in 1600 Japan, when were they born? (p. 5) (EX)
- When Joe thought of a magic trick, it was like it "hit him like a lightning bolt." (p. 51) What does this expression mean? Draw a picture of Joe that illustrates this expression. (DL)
- What is funny about the story? What did you think about the plot? How did you like (or dislike) the characters? (E)

CONTEMPORARY REALISTIC FICTION

Adventure/Survival

Brian's Winter by Gary Paulsen (1996). Bantam Doubleday Dell Publishing Group. In this sequel to *Hatchet* (Paulsen 1987), Brian is not rescued at the end of summer and has to learn how to survive in the hostile, winter environment of the northern Canadian wilderness. Numerous problems face him that are unlike the ones he solved in the summer months. Yet, as the author suggests in his introduction, "Brian had to know summer survival to attempt living in winter" (p. 2).

RL: low fifth grade; IL: fourth–ninth grades; 133 pages

Discussion and Extensions:

- Brian had lived for fifty-four days before he found the survival pack in the plane, and then thirty-five more days through the northern summer (p. 5). How many days from the beginning of the plane crash to the end of summer has Brian survived? How many months? Approximately how many weeks? (EX)
- Paulsen describes Brian as becoming part of nature, a predator, a two-legged wolf (p. 10). What is a predator? (DL) Why had Brian become one? Why did Brian compare himself to a wolf? (I)
- Brian's primary rule was to always pay attention to what was happening (p. 21). What clues or signs did he *not* pay attention to in nature that signaled the coming of winter? (F)
- The author describes a number of problems that Brian must solve in order to survive the winter. How did Brian solve the problem of clothing? Finding food? Moving his feet through the snow? (F)
- Brian says that he had learned that all living things wanted to live (p. 10). What do you think about Brian hunting for food? Could he have done anything else to keep from starving? (CR) What would you have done in Brian's place? (PC)
- "The snow was dry, like crystallized flour or sugar, and seemed to flow away from his legs as he walked" (p. 99). What does crystallized flour or sugar look like? What other comparisons can you make to describe winter snow? (DL)
- What problems do you think Brian might have when he returns to civilization? (I)

Gleam and Glow by Eve Bunting (2001). New York: Harcourt. Simple text illustrated with rich oil paintings by Peter Sylvada describe the events in the life of a family forced to leave their home because of war. When the children are given goldfish by a fleeing neighbor, Marina and Viktor must leave them behind when they escape with their mother across the border to join their father. When it is finally safe to return, they find their home destroyed but the fish alive and flourishing in the pond where they left them. The story is based on a real life event that happened during the Bosnian war.

RL: second grade; IL: third grade and up; 28 pages

Discussion and Extensions:

- Marina and Viktor's father is fighting in the underground. What is "the underground?" (DL)
- Why did Viktor, Marina, and their mother leave their home? (F) Have you ever had to leave something behind that you cared about? How did you feel? (PC)
- Why did the fish survive? (F)
- What do you think about the story? Are the characters believable? How do you feel about the illustrations? Could the story happen today? (E)
- What questions would you like to ask the author, Viktor, Marina, or their parents? (SQ)

Hatchet by Gary Paulsen (1987) (Newbery Honor). New York: Bradbury Press, Macmillan. After his parent's recent divorce, Brian is to spend the summer with his father and the rest of the year with his mother. He is flying in a small bush plane to meet his father when the pilot suddenly slumps over, having suffered a fatal heart attack. Brian must land the plane and then figure out how to survive until rescuers find him. Paulsen uses familiar vocabulary and descriptive language to tell this popular, suspenseful story of survival in the Canadian wilderness. *Brian's Winter* (1996) and *Brian's Return* (1999) follow this first story.

> RL: low fifth grade; IL: fourth–ninth grades; 195 pages

Discussion and Extensions:

- Make a timeline to describe the important events in Brian's quest to survive (e.g., finding food, discovering how to make fire). (F)
- If you were Brian, would you have done anything differently? (PC)
- Brian was rescued after fifty-four days. During that time, he had lost 17 percent of his body weight, but later gained back 6 percent (p. 192). How much body weight must he now gain to be back at his normal body weight? (EX)
- The author describes Brian's memory of the "Secret" to be "like a knife cutting into him. Slicing deep into him with hate" (p. 31). Why did the author use this comparison? What other words could you use to convey the same meaning? (DL)

- The author describes the porcupine as a slithering, brushing sound (p. 80). Why did he use these adjectives? What other animals fit this description? (DL)
- "Gradually, like sloshing oil, his thoughts settled back and the panic was gone" (p. 54). Why did the author compare sloshing oil to Brian's thoughts? (DL)
- Did Brian grow and develop in this story? If so, in what ways? (E)
- Write a review of *Brian's Winter*. Describe what you like (or dislike) and why. (E)

Friendship/Romance

Pacific Crossing by Gary Soto (1992). Orlando, Fla.: Harcourt. Fourteen-year-old Lincoln Mendoza and his friend, Tony Contreras, travel to Japan as exchange students. Both live with Japanese families and experience their graciousness and friendship. Lincoln continues with martial arts lessons that he began in San Francisco; shares language expressions and customs with his new friend, Mitsuo; and with Mitsuo, saves Mr. Ono from a dangerous spider bite encountered during a camping trip. Spanish and Japanese words are scattered throughout, supporting the story's authenticity about two Mexican American teenagers and their Japanese host families. A short glossary of Spanish and Japanese words and phrases follows the novel.

| RL: low fourth grade; IL: sixth grade and up; 126 pages |

Discussion and Extensions:

- What did Lincoln mean when he told Mr. Ono that he could "eat a horse." (p. 84)? Illustrate the two ways this expression may be interpreted. (DL)
- Lincoln agrees with Mitsuo that they should "blow this place" (p. 65). What did he mean? Why is Mitsuo confused with this language expression? (DL)
- Lincoln tells Mitsuo that when he visits him in America that they can "hang out" together (p. 48). Again, Mitsuo is confused. How would you explain this expression to Mitsuo? Illustrate the expression the way Mitsuo interpreted it and the way Lincoln used it. (DL)

- Compare and contrast Mitsuo and Lincoln. Include similarities and differences in religion, food, homes, parents, baths, and sports. (E)
- Lincoln and Tony prepare frijoles, salsa, and enchiladas for their host families. If you went to Japan, what items would you prepare? (PC)
- If Lincoln did fifty push-ups and a hundred sit-ups in one evening at "kempo," how many will he do in one week, two weeks, and three weeks? Make up your own math problem that refers to an event in the story. (EX)
- What did you think about the story? What did you like about it? Would you change anything? Do you think that the author represented all perspectives? If so, what ways? (E)

Seventh Grade from *Baseball in April and Other Stories* by Gary Soto (1990) (Pura Belpe Award Honor Book). New York: Harcourt. Victor, who speaks Spanish and English, decides to take French as his elective because he hopes to go to France someday. On the first day of class, he meets Teresa, on whom he has a crush. When Mr. Bueller asks the class if anyone can speak French, Victor raises his hand to impress Teresa. The teacher asks Victor to say something in French, and after Victor mumbles a made-up word, Mr. Bueller realizes Victor's problem. A perceptive French teacher keeps Victor's secret and an impressed Teresa asks Victor if he will help her with her French. This is one of eleven short stories, with Spanish phrases sprinkled throughout the text. A glossary of Spanish words and expressions follows the short stories.

> RL: fifth grade;
> IL: third–eighth
> grades; 8 pages

Discussion and Extensions:

- What would you have done in Victor's situation if you were in Mr. Bueller's class and wanted to impress Teresa? Have you had similar experiences trying to impress someone? (PC)
- Why did Mr. Bueller keep Victor's secret? (F)
- Write the story from Teresa's perspective; from Mr. Bueller's perspective. (EX)
- Write a short story describing what has happened by the end of the quarter to Teresa and Victor's friendship. (EX)

- What did you think about the story? Did the Spanish phrases help the story? Were the characters believable? (E)
- What questions do you have? (SQ)

The Friends by Kazumi Yumoto (1992; 1998 U.S. translation). New York: Bantam Doubleday Dell Books for Young Readers. This moving story is about the growing friendship between three twelve-year-old boys and an old man on whom they spy to discover what dying will be like. As the friendship grows and the old man reveals his devastating experiences in the war, the boys embark on a journey that changes everyone. This beautifully written story is about friendship, change, separation, and growing up.

> RL: fifth grade; IL: fifth grade and up; 170 pages

Discussion and Extensions:

- How did the boys change the old man? How did the old man change the boys? (I)
- What did Kawabe mean when he said, "I don't understand anything, so I think that maybe there's some kind of hidden rule somewhere" (p. 85)? (I)
- Why does the author compare rain to a crying baby in the following passage: "The rain has slackened a bit, but continues to fall in sudden spurts and hiccups like a crying baby just before it falls asleep" (p. 101)? (DL)
- What does the author mean when he writes, "Kawabe glares at Yamashita, his black eyes sharp like the pointed ends of a pair of thumbtacks" (p. 38)? What other comparison could you use to describe the same fierce glance? (DL)
- Kiyama wonders how many how many times he has breathed since he was born. He says that if he breathes 800 million times in eighty years, then at twelve he has breathed 120 million times (p. 80). Is he correct? How do you know? (EX)
- What did Kiyama mean when he said, "Living is more than just breathing. So dying must be more, too" (p. 81)? (I)
- How did you feel about the story? Were the characters and events believable? Would you change anything? Write a review for others to read. (E)

- What do you think has happened to the boys three years from now? (P) Write a short epilogue. (EX)

Humor

Cockroach Cooties by Laurence Yep (2000). New York: Hyperion Books for Children. Teddy and his younger brother Bobby try to outwit Arnie, the class bully, by threatening him with Bobby's cockroach, named Hercules. Bobby, a good-natured science lover, teaches his older brother about the value of understanding different perspectives. This is a humorous story written from Teddy's point of view, filled with descriptive language and a number of facts about bugs!

RL: second grade; IL: third–seventh grades; 135 pages

Discussion and Extensions:

- Teddy thinks Arnie's fists look like "the size of hams" (p. 20). What did the author mean? What else could you compare them to? Draw a picture of Arnie and his fists.(DL)
- Why is Arnie such a bully? Find reasons in the story to support your answer. (I) Do you know anyone like Arnie? (PC)
- Why did Teddy say that his younger brother Billy was like "a stone around his neck" (p. 28)? What does this expression mean? Have you ever felt that way about anyone? (DL)
- Teddy says that his brother always "looks at the world through rose-colored glasses" (p. 33). What does this expression mean? Use other words to describe someone like Bobby. Does Bobby remind you of anyone? (DL)
- Bobby explains to Teddy: "Just because something's different doesn't make it a monster" (p. 39). What did Bobby mean? What was he talking about? (I)
- What did you learn about cockroaches? For example, how does their skeleton system differ from ours (p. 40)? What did you learn about spiders? (F)
- What was your favorite part in the story? Would you have changed anything (e.g., the fate of Hercules?) Was the story believable? (E)

Double Fudge by Judy Blume (2002). New York: Penguin Putnam Books. Peter, Fudge (i.e., Farley Drexel Hatcher), little sister Tootsie, and parents visit the Bureau of Printing and Engraving in Washington, D.C., to help Fudge become more realistic about his fascination with money. In the gift shop, they meet long-lost cousins from Hawaii who have a four- year- old son named Farley Drexel, another Fudge! Uncle

> RL: third grade; IL: third–seventh grades; 213 pages

Howie, Aunt Eudora, Fauna and Flora (the Natural Beauties), and Farley Drexel decide to camp out on the Hatcher's living room floor to get better acquainted with the relatives. Peter has problems with the Natural Beauties (who are also twelve years old), Fudge doesn't want another Fudge around, and Uncle Feather (the family's myna bird) mysteriously stops talking. This is the fifth book in the Fudge series, written from Peter's perspective.

Discussion and Extensions:

- What does Peter mean when he says that every year he hopes that know-it-all Sheila Tubman won't be in his class and "every year she's there, like some kind of itch you can't get rid of, no matter how hard you scratch" (p. 5)? (DL)
- Why do you think Fudge is fascinated with money? Find evidence from the story (reread pages 44–48 about Richie Potter's visit). (I) Does Richie remind you of anyone? (PC)
- What does Mr. Fargo mean when he exclaims to Peter that he "let the cat out of the bag" (p. 20)? Write about a situation when you "let the cat out of the bag" or when someone you know did. (DL)
- Peter compares riding in the subway, squeezed between strangers, to a sardine—"like sardines in a can" (p. 49). What does this mean? What other comparisons could Peter have used? (DL)
- What did you think about Uncle Howie, Aunt Eudora, and their children? Were they believable? Would you have changed them in any way? (E)
- Peter visits his friend Jimmy's loft apartment in the city. The ceiling is sixteen feet high. How many inches is this? How many yards? Compare the ceiling to something else of a similar size. (p. 53). Peter's father said that he would return for Peter in an hour and a half. How many minutes is that? What could you do in an hour and a half? (EX)

- Compare *Double Fudge* to *Superfudge* or *Fudge-a-Mania*. Which book do you prefer? Why? (E)

Frindle by Andrew Clements (1996). New York: Simon and Schuster. In this humorous story about a word war between teacher and student, fourth-grader Nick Allen invents the word frindle (to replace the word *pen*) when Mrs. Granger requires him to research his own question—what makes a word a word? Frindle has a life of its own when the word becomes a household name around the country and makes Nick a celebrity in the local newspaper and on national TV.

> RL: high third/low fourth grades; IL: third–seventh grades; 105 pages

Did Mrs. Granger choose to be the villain to encourage her creative, innovative student? The author creates colorful characters and raises questions about what is permanent!

Discussion and Extensions:

- Is the story believable? Can anyone invent a new label for a word? (E)
- Why did Nick call Janet's pen a frindle in the first place? (F)
- What do you think about Mrs. Granger? Is she believable? (E) Did this character remind you of anyone? How would you feel if you had a teacher like Mrs. Granger? (PC)
- The author writes: "There was a frown on her face, but her eyes, her eyes were different—almost happy" (p. 47). Why? What did Mrs. Granger enjoy? (I)
- Make up a word for a familiar object that has the same number of syllables as frindle. Illustrate it. (DL)
- Why did Mrs. Granger choose to be the villain in this battle of wills that Nick describes as a chess game? (I)
- Compare Nick and Mrs. Granger. How are they alike and how do they differ? (E)

Hoot by Carl Hiaasen (2002) (Newbery Honor). New York: Knopf. Because of his father's promotions and federal agent position with the government, Roy Eberhardt has again moved to a new town and is the new boy on the block. Once in Trace Middle School,

> RL: middle fifth grade; IL: sixth–ninth grades; 292 pages

in Coconut Cove, Florida, Roy is harassed by the school bully, Dana
Matherson, and befriended by the independent, towering soccer jock
Beatrice "the Bear" Leep and her runaway, barefoot stepbrother, Mullet Fingers (i.e., Napoleon Bridger). Soon, mysterious acts of vandalism
occur at the construction site of Mother Paula's Pancake House and all
of the clues implicate Mullet. Baby owls and a "hoot" of a problem confront Roy and his new friends.

Discussion and Extensions:

- What did the author mean when he described Officer Delinko as
  not being "the sharpest knife in the drawer" (p. 24)? What does this
  expression mean? (DL) What did the officer do to get this description? (F)
- Hiaasen describes Roy "gulping like a beached trout" (p. 15) after
  running to catch up with Mullet Fingers. Why did he use this expression? Describe a time when you have felt this way. (DL)
- Officer Delinko's supervisor said that he was "going out on a limb"
  to give the bungling officer another chance (p. 219). What did the
  captain (i.e., supervisor) mean? Draw a picture illustrating this idiom. (DL)
- Why was Dana Matherson such a bully? Does the author give you
  any clues? (I) Do you know anyone like him? (PC)
- Why did Roy follow Mullet Fingers in the first place? (I)
- Do you think that Roy and Mullet Fingers were right in their actions to protect the young owls? Could they have done anything
  else? (CR) What would you have done to protect the owls? (PC)
- What happens to Mullet Fingers? (P) Write a short epilogue describing where he goes and what he becomes. (EX)
- Is there really such a thing as a burrowing owl? Search the Internet
  and find out all you can. (R)

Jackson Jones and the Puddle of Thorns by Mary Quattlebaum (1994).
New York: Delacorte Press. Jackson is dismayed when his mother gives
him a garden plot in the Rooter's Community Garden
for his tenth birthday when all he wants is a basketball! Jackson soon has a plan to turn his garden into a
profit. This is a short, illustrated chapter book with

RL: 4.3 IL:
fifth–sixth grades;
113 pages

witty language, colorful and generous characters, and a charming story about friendship, family, and ingenuity.

Discussion and Extensions:

- Jackson describes his tenth birthday as "flattened like a basketball hit by a Mack truck" (p. 16). What did he mean? Describe a time when you have felt like Jackson. (DL)
- Jackson and his friend Reuben are combining their savings to invest in seeds for the garden. Jackson says that he's got his $10 birthday money plus one dollar and eleven cents. Counting in Reuben's savings Jackson figures the total amount to be $13.68 (p. 22). How much did Reuben contribute to the fund to invest in seeds? Illustrate this problem. (EX)
- Jackson surveys hoses, gloves, planters, hoes, and shovels and minishovels for the following prices: $6.95, $4.95, $.89, $8.57 (p. 27). How much would Jackson need to purchase these items? (EX)
- Jackson describes his friend's careful entry into the garden to pick weeds in this way: "Rueben goose-stepped into the garden as if it were cold water" (40). Why did the author use this comparison? What does goose-stepped mean? (DL)
- At the end of the story how did Jackson change? What did he learn? (E)

The Boy Who Lost His Face by Louis Sachar (1989). New York: Random House. David Ballinger cannot stand up to peer pressure or for himself. First, he goes along with Randy, Scott, and Roger who maliciously call Mrs. Bayfield a witch and steal her cane, tip her over in her rocking chair, pour lemonade over her, and break her window. Believing that she has put a curse on only him, David lets it rule his life and subdue his secret admiration for the red-haired Tori Williams. This definitely is a theme that explores the dangers of peer pressure and the importance of sticking up for yourself, of not "losing face."

RL: fourth grade; IL: fifth–ninth grades; 198 pages

Discussion and Extensions:

- The boys approached Mr. Bayfield sitting in a rocking chair in front of her dilapidated three-story house (p. 3). What does "dilapidated" mean? Use another word that will fit in the sentence. (DL)

- David's father stared at him incredulously when David told him that he had given his mother the gesture to see if she knew what it meant (p. 37). What does "incredulously" mean? What other word could the author have used? (DL)
- "As inconspicuously as possible, he zipped his fly" (p. 50). Use the context and predict the meaning of "inconspicuously." Make a word map. Include a synonym and an antonym, two examples, the sentence from the story, and your own sentence. Draw David inconspicuously zipping his fly. (DL)
- David lied to Mo and Larry about stealing the cane. The more he lied, the more it bothered him. "It only bothered him a little at first, but the feeling grew, like Pinocchio's nose, with each lie" (p. 98). What does the expression "like Pinocchio's nose" mean? Where does it come from? Have you ever felt this way? Draw a picture of David or yourself (in a similar situation) with Pinocchio's nose. (DL)
- Why didn't David stand up for himself when Randy, Roger, and Scott bullied him and called him names? (I) If you were David, what would you have done? (PC)
- Mrs. Bayfield asked David who was more to blame, the leaders or the followers (p. 146). What do you think—was David more to blame than Randy, Scott, and Roger? What choices did David have? (CR)
- How did David get his face back? (I)
- What did you think about the story? Were the characters believable? What did you think about David? Would you have changed anything? What did you think about the ending—150 years later? (E)

Identity/ Solving Problems

A *Blue-Eyed Daisy* by Cynthia Rylant (Rylant 1985; Aladdin 2001). New York: Simon and Schuster. Ellie, eleven and going on twelve, is fair and quiet, the youngest of five girls living in a poor mining community. In a simple and eloquent manner, Rylant describes everyday events and a range of feelings and emotions, from a first kiss to an uncle

RL: fourth grade; IL: fourth–seventh grades; 99 pages

going to war to her father's near-fatal pickup accident. This short novel is divided into four parts, fall, winter, spring, and summer; each has three to four chapters that portrays experiences that make Ellie exclaim, "some year" (p. 99).

Discussion and Extensions:

- Compare Ellie to her father. How are they alike and how are they different? (E)
- Why was Ellie's father "a drinking man" (p. 3)? (F) How did his drinking affect Ellie and her sister, her mother? Describe Ellie's father; what are his strengths and weaknesses? Why did Ellie feel closer to her father than her mother? (I)
- Why was Ellie's valentine from James so special? (I)
- Find information in the story that describes living conditions, health, and income. (F) How do these factors affect Ellie and her family? (I)
- How did Ellie feel about her uncle becoming a soldier? About going to her first dance? About going hunting? About her teeth? (I)
- What did you think about the story? What did you like? Would you change anything? Did anything surprise you? (E)

Because of Winn-Dixie by Kate DiCamillo (2000). Cambridge, Mass.: Candlewick Press. Ten-year-old India Opal Buloni finds a homeless dog that she names Winn-Dixie. The dog with the winning smile enables Opal, her preacher father, and her special friends (Miss Franny, pinched-face Amanda, Otis, Sweetie Pie, Gloria Dump and Stevie, and Dunlap) to come together at a garden party to celebrate friendship and enjoy the special sweet and sad Littmus Lozenge candies. Opal discovers that, like candy, life can be sweet and sad, that it is important to "love what you've got while you've got it" (p. 167), and that sometimes everyone is lonely.

> RL: third grade/low fourth grade; IL: third–sixth grades; 182 pages

Discussion and Extensions:

- Opal asks her father to describe ten things about her mother. List ten things that describe Opal. (F) Select a favorite pet, or person, and list ten important characteristics. (PC)

- Why did the author create a character like Gloria Dump? Is she a believable character? What was her message? (E)
- Who was Littmus W. Block and why was he important to the story? (E)
- What does "melancholy" mean? Reread page 126. Describe a time when you have felt melancholy. (DL)
- What did you like about the story? Would you change anything? Did you like the characters? Were they believable? Did Opal change over the course of the story? Did her father change? What did you think about the ending? Would you have changed anything? (E)

Egg-Drop Blues by Jacqueline Turner Banks (1995). New York: Houghton Mifflin. Judge Jenkins has reading problems and has been diagnosed with dyslexia. While family and school are concerned that Judge receive proper academic support (such as sending him to another school), he still is in danger of failing science unless he raises his D grade. Coercing his twin brother, Jury, into entering the National Science Einstein Rally to earn extra science points, Judge and his brother pull off the difficult egg-drop event.

RL: fifth grade; IL: fifth–ninth grades; 120 pages

Discussion and Extensions:

- Judge has difficulty reading small words and remembering information. What strategies does he use to help his memory (p. 40)? What strategies does he use for taking a test (p. 77)? (F)
- Judge and Jury must design an egg container that will leave the egg intact when dropped from a distance of twelve feet (p. 40). Predict a distance of twelve feet. (P) Then measure the distance to see how close you are to your prediction. (EX)
- If Judge has two dozen eggs and crushes one egg each time he drops it for the first six times, how many eggs will he have left? (EX)
- Judge and Jury's mother is working "mandatory" overtime. What does this word mean? (DL)
- Jury tells Judge that just because his twin has dyslexia, he won't stop calling him names. He then remarks, "To thine own self be

true" (p. 55). What does he mean by this expression? Where did Jury find the expression? (DL)

- Jury bet Randall and Dan $5.00 that he and Jury would place higher than Randall in the egg contest. Then he raised the bet to $10.00 (p. 60). How much did he raise it? If he doubled that amount (i.e., $10.00), how much money would he need? (EX)
- What did Jury mean when he said that Judge always wore "his heart on his sleeve" (p. 43)? Do you know anyone who wears their heart on their sleeve? Draw this expression. (DL)
- How did Judge and Jury win the egg-drop contest? (F)

Handbook for Boys by Walter Dean Myers (2002). New York: Viking. Told in first person from the perspective of sixteen-year-old Jimmy Lynch, who has been charged with assault on a fellow classmate, Myers's short, poignant novel describes the positive impact that one mentor/supervisor has on the lives of two young offenders. The Duke is given permission to supervise Jimmy and Kevin in his barbershop (Duke's Place) in lieu of the two boys being sent to a juvenile detention facility. As Jimmy works in Duke's Place, he meets colorful patrons of the barbershop, learns to appreciate the wisdom of Duke and his two old friends, Caps and Mr. M., and considers the possibilities of living a "successful life."

RL: third grade;
IL: fifth grade and up; 179 pages

Discussion and Extensions:

- Compare and contrast Jimmy and Kevin. How are they alike and how are they different? (E)
- What was the Duke like? Why do you think he wanted to help Kenny and Jimmy? (I)
- What do you think of the Duke's three Rules for Success (p. 66)? Would they help someone be successful today? Why or why not? (E)
- Why was Peter the Grape successful? (F)
- What choices did Kevin have when he "screwed up" (pp. 166–75)? (F)
- How did Jimmy change over the course of the story? (E)
- What did you think about the story? Why did the author use a barbershop as the setting? Was the story believable? Did you like the

characters? What was the theme or main idea in the story? Was it important? In what way? (E)
- What questions do you have for the Duke, Kevin, or Jimmy? (SQ)

It Doesn't Have to Be This Way: A Barrio Story by Luis J. Rodriguez (1999). San Francisco, Calif.: Children's Book Press. Ten-year-old Ramón "Monchi" is invited to be a member of the Pee Wee gang, but first he must prove himself. Following instructions, Ramón steals a bike, and is ready to become a gang member when his twelve-year-old cousin, Dreamer, intervenes. A near-tragic accident helps Ramón realize

> RL: third grade;
> IL: fifth–ninth
> grades; 31 pages

that he needn't join the gang; "It doesn't have to be this way." The picture book is written in English and Spanish and accompanied by rich, realistic paintings.

Discussion and Extensions:

- Why did Ramón want to be in the gang? What choices did he have? (I)
- Have you ever felt like Ramón, pressured to do something you didn't want to do? What would you have done if you were Ramón? (PC)
- How did Ramón feel when he stole the bike? (I)
- If Dreamer had not been shot, do you think Ramón would have joined the gang? Why or why not? (I)
- What do you think about the story? What is the main idea or theme? Is it important today? What do you like about the illustrations? How do they help tell the story? (E)

Joey Pigza Loses Control by Jack Gantos (2000). New York: Farrar, Straus and Giroux. With his mom's misgivings, Joey and his dog, Pablo, are spending the summer with his dad and grandma. Like Joey, Joey's dad is "wired." While Joey has new meds (medicine) and strategies for his behavior, his dad has other plans for Joey: to get off his meds, to pitch a winning game in the Athletic League baseball tournament, and to go

> RL: fourth grade;
> IL: third–eighth
> grade; 196 pages

on to the big leagues to be the success that he never was. When Joey takes off his patches and his dad starts drinking, life gets complicated and Joey wants to go home. This book follows *Joey Pigza Swallowed the Key*, Gantos's humorous story about a well-intentioned, hyperactive boy who wants to succeed.

Discussion and Extensions:

- Compare and contrast Joey with his father. What are the similarities and what are the differences? (E)
- What did Joey's dad mean when he said, "Heck, giving you medicine is like giving a fish more water" (p. 94)? What else could he have said? (DL)
- What did Joey mean when he said, "I opened one eye like it was a periscope going up and scanning the room for safety" (p. 97)? Draw a picture of Joey that represents this description. (DL)
- Did Joey need his medicine? Find examples to support your answer. (I)
- How did Joey change over the course of the story? What did he learn? (E)
- What did you think about the story? Would you have changed anything? (E)

Joey Pigza Swallowed the Key by Jack Gantos (1998) (National Book Award Finalist). New York: HarperTrophy. This is the first of three humorous stories that describe the well-intentioned, hyperactive, likeable, Joey Pigza. Joey is "wired" and numerous accidents, such as cutting off the tip of Maria Dombrowski's nose with Mrs. Maxy's scissors, leads to a six-week suspension and an assessment at the Lancaster County Special Education Center. Help is on the way, and with the support of "Special Ed" (i.e., Mr. Vanness) and new meds, Joey learns how to make the right decisions, gets a second chance in Mrs. Maxy's class, and a new dog, Pablo. The reader is introduced to multifaceted characters with strengths and weaknesses and who have extended roles in books two and three.

> RL: high third grade; IL: third–eighth grade; 154 pages

Discussion and Extensions:

- When Joey was sent to the special education room and asked to sit in the Big Quiet Chair, he looked calm on the outside but inside felt "like a big bottle of warm Coke when you drop it in the grocery store and it begins to fizz out the top like a bomb about to blow" (p. 38). What did the author mean? What else could you say in the following sentence: "When Joey sat in the Big Quiet Chair he felt like . . . ." Draw a picture of how Joey felt. Have you ever felt this way? (DL)

- How does Joey feel about his mom? Reread page 79, chapter 7. (I)
- Why do you think Joey's mom said that it was easier chasing after Joey's dad than chasing after Joey? (p. 108) (I)
- Joey's mom described his grandma as "tough as old ship leather" (p. 29). What does that expression mean? What else could you compare grandma to? Do you know anyone who is "tough as old ship leather?" (DL)
- Why did Joey love his grandma even though she made him act like a dog and told him that his mother was returning home? Reread chapter 12. (I)
- Why did Joey swallow the key? (F)
- When Joey had his first interview with Special Ed, he was frightened and thought that "nothing was scarier than me knowing something was wrong inside me. . . I was scary to my self." (p. 99) What did Joey mean? (I) Have you ever felt this way? (PC)
- Write a bio poem about Joey. What are his fears? Accomplishments? (EX)

Just Juice by Karen Hesse (1998). New York: Scholastic. Juice, age nine and repeating the fourth grade, hates school. "I don't much care for school, and school, well, it cares even less for me" (p. 2). Juice and her father can't read, and both have kept their secrets from each other, Juice's mother, and four sisters. Pa disregards letters telling him that the house has been sold to pay unpaid back taxes and that he has until September to make up the owed money. Both Pa and Juice like to work with their hands. Pa has lost his job, but discovers that he can sell objects that he makes out of metal. Juice learns that she is not stupid when she reads Ma's sugar level and provides crucial medication that saves her diabetic mother's life and that of her newborn sister. This moving book is about family strength, hidden talents, and the impact of poverty and illiteracy.

RL: fourth grade; IL: third–sixth grades; 138 pages

Discussion and Extensions:

- "I am plain stupid when it comes to reading. Everybody else gets it but reading is pure torture for me" (p. 20). "No one believes how hard I try. No matter what I do, it's never enough" (p. 44). What would it feel like to be Juice? Have you ever experienced anything similar to what Juice experienced? (PC)
- Who was Geneva and how did she help the Faulstich family? (F)
- What did Juice mean when she said, "But with Pa not working at all, life is rough as a cob" (p. 10)? (DL)
- How did Pa's not being able to read contribute to the family's problems? (F)
- What were Juice's strengths and weaknesses? How did she change? (E)
- What do you think will happen to Juice and her family? (P) Write an epilogue or chapter 20 entitled "What happens next." (EX)
- How did poverty affect Juice and her family? Do you think they would have had similar problems living in a city? Would they receive help? Why or why not? (CR)

Locomotion by Jacqueline Woodson (2003). New York: G. P. Putnam's Sons. Woodson writes a sensitive, moving novel in the form of poetry written by Lonnie, a gifted eleven-year-old orphan. Lonnie's parents were killed in an electrical house fire, leaving him and his younger sister, Lili. Lili is adopted and Lonnie is placed in a foster home under the care of Miss Edna. Lonnie's poetry expresses a range of feelings, some only a few lines (e.g., "Georgia," p. 40), while others portray a longer chain of events and observations ("Birth," p. 74; "The Fire," p. 86; "LaTenya," p. 60; and four poems about the "New Boy," pp. 29, 41, 72, and 78). Encouraged by his teacher, Ms. Marcus, who says he has a gift, Lonnie writes his magical words.

> RL: NA; IL: fifth grade and up; 100 pages, 60 poems

Discussion and Extensions:

- How did Lonnie's feelings about the "New Boy" change from his first poem, "New Boy" (p. 29) to his last poem, "Clyde Poem I: Down South," p. 90? (I)

- Lonnie describes the New Boy in "New Boy" (p. 30). Lonnie says the New boy is "looking like he wish he could just melt right on outa the room" (p. 30). What does Lonnie mean? How does the New boy feel? Have you ever felt like you wanted to "melt right out of the room?" (DL) What would you have done if you were in the class with the New Boy? What would you have said or done? (PC)
- What makes the New Boy (Clyde) special in "New Boy, Poem IV" (p. 71)? (F)
- Read Lonnie's list poem ("List Poem," p. 33). Make a list of things that are important to you. Write a list poem like Lonnie's. (EX)
- Read "Failing" (p. 28). Why does Lonnie compare math to people lying? (I)
- What do you think about the book? Do you like Lonnie's poems? Would you recommend it to others? Write a short review for classmates. (E)

Miracle's Boys by Jacqueline Woodson (2000) (Coretta Scott King Award). New York: G. P. Putnam's Sons. Lafayette (age 12), Charlie (age 15), and Tyree (age 22) must figure out how to stay together after the death of their father and recent death of their mother. Charlie has spent three years in a reform school for holding up a candy store and is on probation. Another offense by Charlie, and Tyree will lose custody of his two younger brothers. This is a moving story of Lafayette, who feels responsible for his mother's death; Tyree, who gives up the prospect of going to college to take care of his two brothers; and Charlie, who thinks that he is the bad one, the one who always messes up.

RL: fourth grade; IL: sixth grade and above; 131 pages

Discussion and Extensions:

- Compare the three brothers. What are their strengths and weaknesses? How are they similar and different? (E)
- Why does Lafayette call Charlie "Newcharlie"? (I)
- Lafayette feels that he was to blame for his mother's death and Tyree feels that he is to blame for his father's death. Why? (I)
- Charlie feels angry. Why? (I) How would you feel if you were Charlie? (PC)

- What does "got a monkey on their back" mean (see p. 81)? Have you ever felt that you had a monkey on your back? Illustrate this expression. (DL)
- How do you feel about the book? What did you like? Would you change anything? Did the brothers change in the story? Were they believable characters? (E)
- Predict what happens to the boys in the following year. (P) Write chapter 18. (EX)

Monster by Walter Dean Myers (1999) (Coretta Scott King Award; National Book Award Finalist). New York: HarperCollins. Steve Harmon is on trial for felony murder. In order to survive the fear, tension, and loneliness of his confinement in the Manhattan Detention Center, Steve writes a screenplay that describes his ordeal and the events that led up to his murder conviction. Myers's riveting story uses flashbacks to explore Steve's conscience, his guilt or innocence, as he changes from bystander to player in a story that is quickly spiraling out of control.

RL: fourth grade; IL: sixth grade and up; 281 pages

Discussion and Extensions:

- Prosecutor Ms. Petrocelli says that Steve Harmon has made a moral decision (p. 270). What decisions did Steve make? Why did he make them? (I) Could he have done anything differently to change the outcome of the robbery? (CR) What would you have done if you were Steve Harmon the night of the robbery? (PC)
- Compare and contrast Steve and Bobo. How are they alike and how are they different? Do these characters remind you of anyone? (E)
- Compare Sandra Petrocelli (prosecutor) and Kathy O'Brien (defense attorney). Are there any similarities or differences in these characters? (E)
- What is the main idea or theme? Do you think that it is important? Why? (E)
- Make a story map that includes the two settings (journal notes and courtroom) and events that take place in each. (F)

- What did you think about the story? Would you have changed anything? Were the characters and events believable? Did Steve Harmon change over the course of the story? In what ways? (E)
- What questions would you like to ask Steve Harmon? (SQ)

Pictures of Hollis Woods by Patricia Reilly Giff (2002). New York: Random House. Hollis Woods, soon to be twelve, has run away from numerous foster homes, but her latest one with the Regan family seems to fit. Izzy, the Old Man, and Steven want her to stay and she does, too, until the accident—which she thinks is her fault. Hollis runs away, determined not to bring the Regan family any harm. This time, the agency places her with Josie Cahill, a retired, eccentric artist with whom she quickly forms a loving bond. All seems well until Josie starts forgetting things, and the agency makes arrangements to move Hollis to another placement. This time Hollis takes Josie with her, fleeing to the Regans' mountain cabin, since she fears that the old woman cannot survive alone. Knowing that the cabin has been closed for the winter, Hollis plans to stay there with Josie until she can get help for her old friend. The story is structured with chapters alternating between the present and past, with flashbacks described in terms of colors and drawings made by a talented and lonely twelve-year-old. Each flashback chapter presents rich opportunities for prediction.

RL: third grade; IL: sixth–ninth grade; 166 pages

Discussion and Extensions:

- At the end of each flashback chapter, predict what has happened between Hollis and the Regan family. Why did she leave a family that wanted her to stay? (I)
- Hollis remarked that with the Regans she was a different person. "I was a new person with the Old Man, with Izzy, with Steven. It was as if the angry Hollis were seeping right out of my bones, leaving chocolate as soft as that sticky Hershey bar" (p. 40). What did Hollis mean? Why did she feel like a different person? What did the Regans do to make her feel this way? (I) Have you ever felt as angry as Hollis? Have you ever felt as good, like a sticky Hershey bar? (PC)
- Hollis feels ecstatic, jubilant with the Regans, and plans to go to the top of the mountain to shout that she will soon have a family. She

uses all of her colors—"yellow and oranges, pinks and blues. I drew purple shoes on my feet and wings on my shoulders" (p. 110). Draw a picture of Hollis on top of the mountain. Use your own colors and draw a picture of a time when you felt "jubilant." (EX)

- How did Hollis change over the course of the story? What were her strengths? What were her weaknesses? (E)
- Why did Hollis dislike the foster home agency people, such as the "Mustard" woman, and make up names to call them? (I)
- When Mr. Regan visited her at the agency, Hollis wouldn't look at him. After she left, she remarked to Emmy, "You want tough? I'll show you tough" (p. 146). What did Hollis mean? Why do you think she said this? (I)
- How do you feel about the chapter flashbacks? Do you like them or are they confusing? Do they help the story? (E)

Searching for David's Heart by Cherie Bennett (1998). New York: Scholastic. Darcy Deeton's older brother David is her hero. When David brings home a girlfriend to share Darcy's twelfth birthday, a jealous Darcy verbally lashes out at her brother and his girlfriend, Jayne. When she follows her brother and Jayne to the park to apologize, she overhears the couple talking about how her birthday gift (a heart necklace identical to the one that David gave Jayne) was Jayne's idea. Angrily, Darcy screams that she hates them both and races out of the park and across the street, with David close behind. Darcy dodges the oncoming traffic but David is hit and never regains consciousness. Feeling heartbroken and responsible for David's subsequent death, Darcy believes that if she finds the individual that has been given David's transplanted heart, she will also find something of David. She secretly leaves home with her friend, Sam, and begins an adventure that ends in hope and healing for the Deeton family.

> RL: fifth grade; IL: fifth–ninth grades; 220 pages

Discussion and Extensions:

- When David said that their grandmother, Meemaw, didn't like it that no one talked to her, Darcy gave her brother a withering look (p. 24). What kind of look is a "withering" look? Use another adjective that suggests the same meaning. Create a word map that includes the word, multiple meanings (i.e., withering plant, withering look), the sentence in the story, and several of your own sentences. Draw someone with a withering look. (DL)

- What do you think about Darcy's behavior to her invalid grandmother? David's behavior to her grandmother? Which one would you be more like? Why? (PC)
- Why did Darcy keep her secret about David's accident to herself? When and why did she finally share it with others? (F)
- What do you think about Darcy? Do you like her? What are her strengths and her weaknesses? (E)
- If Sam bought a hamburger for $3.50, a shake for $1.25, and French fries for $2.00, how much change would he receive from a $10 bill? (EX)
- Make a graphic organizer or "map" that illustrates the major events that happen to Darcy and Sam on their bus ride to Florida. Refer to the text for specific information. (F)
- Illustrate your feelings about the story. Use colors or paint to represent what you felt the story was about. (EX)
- What has happened to Darcy, Sam, and Winston in twelve years? (P) Write an epilogue that briefly describes what they are doing. (EX)

The Jacket by Andrew Clements (2002). New York: Simon and Schuster. When Philip, a tall sixth grader, sees a boy in his younger brother's jacket, he assumes it is stolen. A fight begins and both Philip and an angry Daniel are taken to the principal's office. Philip soon recognizes his mistake and begins looking more closely at himself and his family. Is he prejudiced? Would he have made the same mistake if Daniel had been white? This easy-to-read book explores prejudices, differences, and the universality of human experiences from Clement's believable characters: Daniel, Philip, Daniel's grandma Lucy, and Philip's parents.

> RL: low second grade; IL: third–seventh grades; 89 pages

Discussion and Extensions:

- What do you think about Philip's reaction to seeing Daniel in a jacket that looked like his brother's jacket? What about Daniel's behavior? (CR) What would you have done if you were Philip? If you were Daniel? (PC)

- Why did Philip tell ask his mom, "How come you never told me I was prejudiced?" (p. 37). Do you think he was prejudiced? (CR)
- Why did Daniel offer to buy Philip's ice cream? (I) What would you have done? (PC)
- Why did Lucy call Philip's mom by her first name and his father by his last name? What does Philip's father think and say that would make Lucy feel uncomfortable and Philip describe him as being prejudiced? (CR)
- Philip said that being friends with everyone and being someone's friend were two different things (p. 18). What did he mean? (I)
- Compare and contrast Philip and Daniel. How were they alike? How were they different? (E)
- Do you think the characters were realistic? How were they believable? (E)
- How did Philip grow and develop throughout the story? How did Daniel change? (E) Do you think it is possible that they became friends? Would they sit by each other in the lunch room or visit or be invited to each other's homes? Or would they only be friendly? (CR)

The Janitor's Boy by Andrew Clements (2000). New York: Simon and Schuster. Fifth-grader Jack Rankin is embarrassed that his father is a janitor. Angered by classmates' cruel taunts about being "the janitor's son," Jack decides to get even with his father by sticking wads of soft, smelly chewing gum underneath a table and chair in the music room. An angry vice principal (who does not realize that Jack's father is the head custodian) informs Jack that he is to help the head custodian clean up gum for three weeks. While cleaning up gum, a begrudging and curious Jack steals two janitor keys, one of which opens up a door to a steam tunnel that extend miles underneath the ground. The trouble is, when Jack wants out he realizes that he doesn't have the correct key to open the tunnel door from the inside! A good story with fast-paced events explores family relationships, respect, friendship, responsibility, and helping others.

> RL: low fourth grade; IL: third–seventh grade; 140 pages

Discussion and Extensions:

- Compare and contrast Jack with his dad. What are the similarities? What are the differences? (E)
- In second grade, Jack said that he wanted to be a janitor like his dad. The kids laughed and now in fifth grade, the teasing is more hurtful and malicious. What could you do if you were in Jack's class and your group teased Jack? What would you do? (PC)
- Jack thought that Kirk Dorfmann was a "walking fashion ad" (p. 16). What did he mean? How did Kirk look? Do you know anyone who fits this description? (DL)
- What do you think about Jack's behavior in defacing a chair and table with gum to "get back" at his father? What other choices did Jack have? (CR)
- Jack climbed five flights with ten stairs per flight to reach the tower landing. How many stairs did Jack walk up to reach the top of the tower? Illustrate this problem. (EX)
- There are 855 folding seats in the auditorium. If gum is on one third of the seats, how many seats will Jack have to clean? How did you arrive at your answer? (EX)
- What did Jack learn about his father? (F) How did his father's experiences (home and war experiences) affect his father's life? (I)
- Would you have changed anything in the story? What did you like about it? What is the main idea or theme? Is it important? Did anything bother you? (E)

The Skin I'm In by Sharon Flake (1998). New York: Hyperion Paperbacks for Children. Maleeka, a seventh-grade student at McClenton Middle School, thinks she and the new teacher are freaks: she because of her very black skin and handmade clothes, and Miss Sanders with the "giant white stain spread halfway across her face like somebody tossed acid on it or something" (p. 1). Throughout this gripping book, Maleeka struggles

> RL: fifth grade; IL: seventh grade and up; 171 pages

to find her identity, understand her need to fit in, her dependent relationship with popular bully Charlese, her growing friendship with Miss Sanders (the teacher who supports Maleeka's intellect and writing ability), and discovers the dire consequences of following along.

Discussion and Extensions:

- Why did Maleeka "hang out" with Char (Charlese)? Why did Char have the power to influence Maleeka throughout the story? (I)
- Compare and contrast Maleeka and Char, their personalities and home life. (E)
- Maleeka describes Char's eyes as being cold and hard, like flat black skipping rocks at the bottom of the creek (p. 141). Why did the author use these words? Think of another comparison to describe Char's eyes. (DL)
- Why did Maleeka fail to stand up to Char when Charlese and the twins wanted to pay back Miss Sanders? What choices did Maleeka have? (I) What would you have done in the same situation? (PC)
- Why did John-John tease Maleeka? Support your answer with evidence from the story. (I)
- What did you think about the story? Where the characters believable? What is the main idea or theme? Is it important? Would you have changed anything? (E) Write a review for other readers. (EX)

Vanishing by Bruce Brookes (1999). New York: HarperCollins. Eleven-year-old Alice has quit eating. Her natural father has told her that she must live with her mother, who drinks too much, and her new stepfather, whom she thinks is a bully. Alice feels that it is easier to float away in her hospital room where no one can reach rather than go on living. Then she becomes friends with Rex, a patient in remission from a critical illness. When Rex slips out of remission and is moved to another location in the hospital, Alice must gain back her energy to find him and, in doing so, discovers that living is worth the effort after all.

RL: third grade; IL: fifth grade and up; 103 pages

Discussion and Extensions:

- Why did Alice quit eating? What were her other choices? (I) What would you have done in her place? (PC)
- What did Rex mean when he said, "You, Alice, are the man" (p. 14). (DL)
- "She began to rise off the mattress, and she knew it was okay, she was on her way, the lightness was coming. . . . Finally, the bubbles

popped and she was that light gas itself, rising. But even the gas was too heavy, and it faded away. After that, there was nothing to do but vanish." (79, 80). Draw a picture of Alice that illustrates her feeling of "vanishing." (EX)

- How did Rex help Alice? Did Alice help Rex as well? (I)
- How did you feel about the book? What did you like? What would you change? What is the major theme? Is it important? Did Alice change in the story? Is she a believable character? Is Rex? Would you recommend the book to another reader? (E) Use colors or paints to illustrate your feeling about the story. (EX)
- What questions do you have about the story? (SQ)
- What happened to Alice, Nat, Alice's mother? Rex's parents? (P) Write an epilogue. (EX)

What Would Joey Do? by Jack Gantos (2002). New York: Farrar, Straus and Giroux. Joey tries to make things better in a dysfunctional family that includes his divorced parents and ailing grandmother. When Joey's dad ("wired" like Joey and his grandmother) returns for Thanksgiving, events quickly get out of control. Colorful characters with strengths and weaknesses include hyperactive, good-intentioned Joey; his immature, hyperactive dad; his loving and overreactive mother and her good-natured boyfriend, Booth;

> RL: low fourth grade; IL: third–eighth grade; 229 pages

Joey's crusty grandma with emphysema; and Oliva Lapp (the blind, homeschooled neighbor with whom Joey is paired, and who tries to be independent no matter who gets in her way!). This is the third book about Joey Pigza.

Discussion and Extensions:

- When Joey's mom jams a broom handle into the spokes of his dad's motorcycle, his dad is "shot forward yowling like a cat blasted out of a cannon" (p. 13). Why did the author make this comparison? Close your eyes and describe what you see. Illustrate it. (DL)
- "Grandma had rolled her bloodshot eyes more times than a losing slot machine and was shuffling her way toward the sofa to hide behind her curtain and smoke a cigarette" (p. 27). Why did the author compare grandma's eyes to a losing slot machine? What does

"shuffling" mean? What other adjective could he use? (DL) Draw a picture of grandma. (EX)

- What does Olivia mean when she says, "Joey, you're so blind you can't see this has nothing to do with you. It's about me" (p. 147). (DL)
- Why was Joey's relationship with his grandma so important? (I) How would you have felt if you were Joey? (PC)
- What do you think about the story? Would you have changed anything—for example, Booth leaving or grandma dying? What did you think about Joey? Is Joey a believable character? Why or why not? (E)
- Use a Venn diagram and compare this book to another book about Joey Pigza. Which book did you like better? Why? (E)

Mystery

Dead Letter, A Herculeah Jones Mystery by Betsy Byars (1996). New York: Penguin Group. Herculeah buys a secondhand fur coat and finds a foreboding letter hidden away in the pocket lining. The letter, a cry for help from a soon-to-be murder victim, makes Herculeah's hair frizzle (a sign of danger!) and starts the young detective and her friend Meat on a journey to find the murderer. A suspicious house key, a faded telephone number, a menacing black car, and a killer Doberman are a few of the clues and suspenseful events that befall the courageous young heroine. This series is full of cliffhanger events and descriptive, colorful language.

> RL: low fourth grade; IL: third–seventh grade; 147 pages

Discussion and Extensions:

- Make a timeline to show the events and clues that lead Herculeah and Meat to the killer. (F)
- What was the motive? (F)
- How did Herculeah escape the dangerous Doberman? (F)
- Substitute your own descriptive words for the italicized words: "Herculeah *inched* slowly toward the door. Her heart *pounded*. Her legs were like *rubber*, too weak to support her. She was aware that at any moment the Doberman could turn and attack" (p. 136). (DL)

- Read the following description of the trees in Dead Oaks: "Then there was only the rustling of the trees in the early evening breeze, a sorrowful sound, as if they mourned their fallen friends" (p. 59). How does this description make you feel? Illustrate the setting that the author has created with her words. (DL)
- "Another chill went up her spine. Someone walking on my grave. That was just an old expression, she reminded herself. Nothing to it" (p. 63). What does the expression "someone walking on my grave" mean? Have you ever felt this way? (DL)
- Read the author's vivid description of Roger Cole and draw a picture of this scheming, dangerous character. "The man getting out of the black car was tall and handsome, his smile Hollywood white, his eyes as blue as his cashmere sweater" (p. 97). (EX)
- What did you like about the story? (E) Write a review for another reader. (EX)

Death's Door, A Herculeah Jones Mystery by Betsy Byars (1997). New York: Penguin Group. As Herculeah and her friend Meat (wearing his Uncle Neiman's cowboy hat that has a feather) are walking down the street, a hired gunman is taking aim. His job? To kill the man in the cowboy hat! As the bullet zings through the air, Herculeah pushes Meat aside and the mystery begins. Why does the hired killer want

RL: third grade; IL: third–seventh grade; 133 pages

Meat's Uncle Neiman dead? How does Herculeah find herself face-to-face with the gunman? What clue does Meat find in the newspaper? These are a few of the puzzles in Byars's fast-paced mystery.

Discussion and Extensions:

- Who is the Bull? (pp. 9, 10) (F) Draw your image of this character. (EX)
- What type of person is Uncle Neiman? (I) Do you know anyone like him? (PC)
- "He had landed hard on his face and elbows—two of his most vulnerable spots—and Herculeah had cushioned her fall by landing on him" (pp. 29–30). What does vulnerable mean? Describe a situation when you have felt vulnerable. (DL)
- Who hired the Bull and why? (F)

- What do you think about Meat? Is he a believable character? Do you like him? Why or why not? Would you like a friend like him? (E)
- What clues did Meat find in the newspaper? (F)
- What would happen if the police did not catch the Bull? (P) Rewrite the ending. (EX)

Disappearing Acts, A Herculeah Jones Mystery by Betsy Byars (1998). New York: Penguin Group. This time Meat finds a girl's body in a guys' bathroom in the comedy club Funny Bonz! A blue wallet, a tube of lipstick, a ponytail, and undeveloped film in a camera from a secondhand store are events that spearhead two plots: a murder and the whereabouts of Meat's missing father. This is the third mystery in the *Herculeah Jones* series.

> RL: third grade;
> IL: third–seventh
> grades; 120 pages

Discussion and Extensions:

- Compare and contrast Meat and Herculeah. How are they similar and how are they different? How does the author make them believable? (E)
- Who are Marcie Mullet and the Macho Man? How are they connected to Meat? (F)
- What do the blue wallet, tube of lipstick, and a ponytail have to do with the murder? What clues lead to Meat's father? (F)
- What do you think about the plot? The characters? The ending? Would you change anything? (E)
- What happens to Meat and his father? (P) Write an epilogue that describes their relationship. (EX)
- Compare *Disappearing Acts* with either *Dead Letter* or *Death's Door*. Which mystery did you prefer? Why? (E)

No More Magic by Avi (1975). New York: Random House. Chris leaves his bicycle out on Halloween night and discovers that it is gone the next morning. Clues lead to the new mysterious neighbor, Muffin, who wears a druid-like woven coat, Chris's best friend Eddie, and the owner of the bike shop, Mr. Bullen. Who is the warlock or witch? Who does

> RL: fourth grade;
> IL: third–seventh
> grades; 138 pages

Chris see flying in front of the moon on his stolen green bike in a check-ered coat? Avi's good story examines the consequences of making accu-sations without evidence or forethought.

Discussion and Extensions:

- Chris tells his brother that "Someday you're going to put your big foot in your mouth" (p. 20). What did he mean? Have you ever felt like you put your foot in your mouth? Draw this expression. (DL)
- Chris calls Muffin's aunt a "real zero" (p. 43). What does he mean? (DL)
- Eddie "sarcastically" tells Chris that he did indeed go to the Hal-loween parade. What does this word mean? (DL) Why did Eddie act this way? Support you answer with facts. (I)
- Chris's mother was "baffled" that she couldn't identity the type of weave in Muffin's coat (p. 39). What does this word mean? Think of a time when you have been baffled. (DL)
- Why did Muffin accuse Eddie of stealing Chris's bike? (I)
- What clues did Chris find that made him suspect Muffin? (F)
- Of the three characters—Eddie, Chris, and Muffin—whom would you like as a best friend? Why? (PC)
- Why did Muffin think that magic was to blame for her parents leav-ing her? (I)

HISTORICAL REALISTIC FICTION

Adventure/Survival

Crispin by Avi (2002) (Newbery Award). New York: Hyperion Books. The setting is in England, 1377 A.D. Crispin, better known as Asta's son, loses his mother and becomes an orphan. Never know-ing his father, Crispin has only an iron cross as a keep-sake. After overhearing a mysterious conversation, ene-mies pronounce Crispin "a wolf's head"—a declaration that allows anyone to kill him on sight. Befriended by a huge, red-haired man called "Bear," Crispin learns the value of friendship and freedom. Col-orful characters include Bear, the conniving Lady Furnival, the evil, power hungry Aycliff, and the ill-fated Father Quinel.

> RL: fifth grade; IL: fifth–ninth grade; 262 pages

Discussion and Extensions:

- Compare living conditions, food, and power structures that the author described in the story to our present day. (E)
- Read the author's description and draw a picture of Bear. (EX)
- Why did Aycliff call Crispin a wolf's head? What secret did the iron cross reveal? (F)
- What was the major theme in the story? Is the theme important today? Could you write the same story using a current time and place? (E)
- Based on the story, predict what happens to Crispin and Bear. (P)
- Did Crispin grow and develop over the course of the story? If so, in what ways? (E)
- What events make the story believable? What did you think about the story? Would you have ended it like the author did? (E)

Freedom's Wings: Corey's Diary, Kentucky to Ohio, 1857 by Sharon Dennis Wyeth (2001) (A Dear American Book). New York: Scholastic. Short diary entries describe the perilous journey of nine-year-old Corey and his mother, Angel, as they escape the Hart family plantation to find Corey's father and freedom in Canada. Corey, who can read and write, keeps a treasured journal that tells about his life as a slave, his father's narrow escape, the courageous people who risk their lives to help his mother and him find escape routes via the Underground Railroad, and his final reunion with his father.

> RL: high second/low third; IL: third–fifth grades; 102 pages with historical notes

Discussion and Extensions:

- How did Corey learn to read and write? Why was this so dangerous? (F)
- Why did Young Bob leave a bottle of ink in a hole in the oak tree for Corey to discover? (F)
- What is the Underground Railroad? Who was part of it? How did slaves and freedom fighters use signs to communicate? (F)
- What did Corey mean when he said, "Underground Railroad be our freedom's wings" (p. 92)? (I)

- What new information can you find about the Underground Railroad on the web? What famous African Americans are associated with the Underground Railroad? (R)
- Make a timeline that shows important events and places in Corey's escape to freedom. (F)

One Candle by Eve Bunting (2002). New York: HarperCollins. This moving picture book story is about a Jewish family's tradition of celebrating Hanukkah. Every year Grandma hollows out a potato and, with Aunt Rose, tells about the dark time they spent in the Buchenwald concentration camp and how they stole one potato to make a Hanukkah candle. Flashbacks explain how the hungry and frightened sisters light the potato using a piece of stolen margarine and a thread from Rose's skirt for a wick to honor Hanukkah. The realistic illustrations—soft color pastels noting the present and black-and-white drawings representing the past—support this story of survival, courage and remembrance.

RL: third grade; IL: third grade and up; 29 pages

Discussion and Extensions:

- How did you feel about the story? What do think about the illustrations? Do they support they story? The artist illustrates some of the events in black and white and other events in color. Why does the artist do this and do you think it helps tell the story? (E)
- Why was the potato so important to Aunt Rose and Grandma? Why did they risk their lives to steal the potato? (F) Do you know anyone like Grandma or Aunt Rose? (PC)
- What is the theme(s) of the story? What main ideas did the author present? (E)
- Do you think the story relates to present-day events? If so, in what ways? (CR)
- What questions do you have about the story? What questions would you like to ask Grandma or Aunt Rose? (SQ)

The Fighting Ground by Avi (1984). New York: HarperCollins. On April 3, 1778, thirteen-year-old Jonathan meets a burly corporal who is recruiting men to fight the British. The young teenager secretly leaves home to fight with the corporal. Within two days, Jonathan sees the grim realities and the ambiguities of war. For example, when Jonathan is captured by three German soldiers, he discovers that it is the corporal, and not the Germans, who are responsible for a French family's death. When he escapes the sleeping Hessians and returns to the Americans, the corporal demands that Jonathan lead him back to capture (and kill) the Germans. Jonathan's choices and the consequences of his actions support the story's strong theme.

> RL: high third grade; IL: third–seventh grades; 152 pages

Discussion and Extensions:

- Why do you think the author wrote the story to take place in only two days? Would the story have been better if it covered more time? Why or why not? (E)
- What do you think about the story? Would you have changed anything? (E)
- After the corporal and his men find and kill the German soldiers, he tells Jonathan that the Hessians killed American soldiers and bayoneted the wounded at Long Island because they were soldiers—like himself and Jonathan. What did he mean when he added, "You were lucky, that's all. There's nothing more to it" (p. 147)? (I)
- What do you think about Jonathan's decision to tell the corporal where the German soldiers were hiding? Do you think he made the right decision? What would you have done if you were Jonathan? (CR)
- What did Jonathan learn and how did he feel after his two days of war? (I)
- Why did the corporal tell Jonathan that the gun that he had borrowed needed returning? (p. 147)? Why did Jonathan smash the gun to pieces? (I)
- How do you think the author feels about war? Why did he portray the corporal and the German soldiers the way he did? Would you have done anything differently? (CR)

The Girl Who Chased Away Sorrow: The Diary of Sarah Nita, a Navajo Girl by Ann Turner (1999). New York: Scholastic. Twelve-year-old Sara

Nita carefully records her grandmother's words as the old woman describes the hardship and bravery of the Navajo Indians during their capture and forced winter walk in 1864 from Arizona to Fort Sumner, New Mexico. Short, descriptive journal entries told from the perspective of the first Sara Nita (also twelve years old) describe believable characters, rich cultural traditions, and the tragic events that end

> RL: high third grade; IL: fourth–ninth grades; 174 pages

with the families' survival and return to their homeland. The author's historical notes and photographs provide additional information surrounding the setting and events of her readable, fascinating historical fiction novel.

Discussion and Extensions:

- Frightened by the swirling smoke arising from her parent's home, Sara Nita describes her reaction: "I open and shut my mouth silently like a caught fish" (p. 20). What does this mean? How did Sara Nita feel? Have you ever felt this way? (DL)
- Half-Alive Man says that White People are made of leftover bad parts, the parts of the weasel and rattlesnake (p. 59). Why did he say this? Did other Navajos share his feelings about the White Men? (I)
- Why was Sarah Nita referred to as the Girl Who Chased Away Sorrow? What did she do? (F)
- How did the author portray feelings and perspectives of Sara Nita, her family, and the white soldiers? Did she present a balanced viewpoint of events and characters, both Indians and whites? (E)
- What was the white powder called "Flaarhh?" Why did the Indians have difficulty eating it? (I)
- How did Sarah Nita find corn for her sick father? (F) What would you have done? (PC)
- What injustices did Sarah, her family, and other Navajos endure? Read the historical notes after the story. On what real events did the author base her story? (F)
- Find out what you can about the Navajo Indians. What is being done to support the Navajos today? (R)

The Journal of Jessie Smoke: A Cherokee Boy by Joseph Bruchac (2001). New York: Scholastic. Written in short journal entries by Jessie Smoke, a young literate Cherokee Indian, Jessie's diary covers a two-year period that describes the forced removal of the Cherokees from their land and their relocation west along what is now known as the Trail of Tears. The betrayal by President Jackson with the Treaty of New Echota and the enforced stay in concentration camps prior to journeying west are a few of the events and injustices described through the sensitive, intelligent eyes of the young Cherokee.

RL: low fifth grade; IL: sixth grade and up; 173 pages

Discussion and Extensions:

- Read the author's historical notes. Who were the Cherokee Indians? How did they differ from other Indian tribes? Why did the white settlers want their land? What treaty forced their removal? (F)
- Describe Jessie Smoke. What was he like? What were his parents like? (F) What did you learn about him from his journal? (I)
- Did the author present perspectives from both the Cherokees and the American government? (CR) How did the author support the events he related in his story in his historical notes? What characters (both Indian and white) represented different viewpoints? (E)
- The author compares the removal of the Cherokees from their homeland as what is known today as "ethnic cleansing." Why does he say this? (I)
- Compare the forced migration of the Cherokee Indians to a similar situation that has occurred in today's world. What are the similarities and differences between the Cherokees and other victims who are forced to leave their homelands? (E) (CR)
- Describe the concentration camps in Georgia and Tennessee. What conditions did Jessie, his mother, and sisters have to endure? (F)
- In the epilogue, the author describes 1839 to 1961 as the Golden Age of the Western Cherokee Nation. Write journal entries from Jessie's perspective that describes his life during this time. (EX)

The Journal of Wong Ming-Chung: A Chinese Miner by Laurence Yep (2000). New York: Scholastic. Yep's fascinating story is constructed around journal entries that describe a year (1851–1852) in the life of twelve-year-old Bright Intelligence, called the Runt because of his small size. Leaving home to meet his Uncle in California, Runt endures a treacherous sea voyage to California and soon learns that foreigners are not welcome by most Americans mining for gold. Runt, who bravely refuses to leave his uncle and the dangers of gold mining, provides readers with a glimpse of the bravery and perseverance of young immigrants that helped to make America strong.

RL: third grade; IL: fourth–eighth grades; 195 pages including the epilogue

Discussion and Extensions:

- Why were Runt and other immigrants treated so badly during the voyage to California and later by the American miners? (F)
- Make a timeline of Runt's voyage from the time he left China to the time he arrived in California, the Golden Mountain. (F)
- The author describes the coming of autumn in the following way: "The leaves litter the ground like old coins" (p. 133). What does he mean? To what else could you compare golden leaves? (DL)
- In what ways did Runt's friend Hiram show his friendship? (F)
- What did Fox mean when he told Runt, "You can tell the quality of a person by the company that person keeps" (p. 149)? (DL)
- Read the epilogue. Why do you think Runt was successful? (I)
- Runt and his uncle endured physical and verbal abuse because they were different. Are there situations today where they would feel uncomfortable? (CR)

Friendship/Romance

Pink and Say by Patricia Polacco (1994). New York: Putnam and Grosset. This is a moving story written and illustrated by Patricia Polacco about Sheldon Curtis (ancestor of Polacco) and Pinkus Alyee, both adolescents fighting for the Union Army. Sheldon (Say) is a deserter from the Ohio Twenty-Fourth and Pinkus (Pink), an African American, fights for the Forty-Eighth Colored. Pink finds Say wounded from a

RL: third grade; IL: fourth–ninth grades; 42 pages

musket shot to the knee and takes him home to be nursed by his mother, Moe Moe Bay. The boys become friends, each sharing special talents, until tragedy strikes and the boys are taken captive by the Confederate Army. The author dedicates her story to the memory of Pinkus Aylee, killed in Andersonville Prison soon after being captured.

Discussion and Extensions:

- Why was Pink and his company not allowed at first to carry guns— and then were given old muskets that jammed and misfired? (I) In what ways does discrimination exist today? (CR)
- Why did the author write from Say's perspective? Would the story have been different from Pink's point of view? (E)
- Why was it against the law to teach slaves to read? How did Pink lean to read? (F)
- What did Moe Moe Bay mean when she told Say that Master Aylee showed him how paper talks? (I)
- Pink's mother was inconsolable when he told her he and Say had to return to the war (p. 23). What does inconsolable mean? Predict the meaning. Look the word up in the dictionary. Make a word map and include synonyms, examples, the sentence from the story, and your own sentence. Draw Moe Moe Bay's expression when Pink told her he was going to return to the war. (DL)
- What did you think about the illustrations? What do you like about them? How do they help tell the story? (E)
- Research the Civil War on the Internet. Find out all you can about Pink's unit, the Forty-Eight Colored. What were the differences between the African American unit and the white units fighting for the Union (e.g., number of soldiers, assignments, weapons, treatment)? What events helped to cause the Civil War? Who were the marauders? (R)

Sarah, Plain and Tall by Patricia MacLachlan (1985) (Newbury Medal). New York: HarperTrophy. This short novel tells the heartwarming story about headstrong Sarah, a "plain and tall" woman from Maine, who comes to live with a widower and his two children for a month's time "to see how it is" (p. 14). Although Sarah misses the sea and its colors, Anna, Caleb, and their father soon win her heart.

RL: third grade; IL: third–seventh grade; 58 pages

Discussion and Extensions:

- Why does Sarah love and miss the sea? Support your answer with references from the book. (F)
- Does the book remind you of anything? Have you ever moved, or were separated from something that you cared about? How did you feel? (PC)
- Describe Sarah—physically, mentally, and how she behaved on Pa's farm. Do you know anyone like Sarah? (PC)
- Pa says: "Sarah is Sarah. She does things her way, you know" (p. 35). What did he mean? (I)
- How did Sarah bring the sea to the prairie? (F)
- Draw a favorite part or how you feel about the story. Choose colors that support your feelings. (PC)
- What do you like about the story, the characters? Is there anything you would change? (E) Write a review for classmates. (EX)

Identity/Solving Problems

Keeper of the Doves by Betsy Byars (2002). New York: Viking. Written in the first person from the perspective of young Amen, Byars tells the story about a family in the late 1800s and how judgments and appearances can deceive. Mr. Tominski is the elusive, childlike "keeper of the doves." Amen's twin sisters call him a murderer when they suspect him of killing the family dog. Amen's father calls him family. This is a short, sensitive novel that examines multiple perspectives, growing up, and the complexity of human relations.

> RL: high third/low fourth; IL: third–seventh grades; 121 pages

Discussion and Extensions:

- The author set the book in the late 1800s. What was different about living in this time? Was anything the same? Where attitudes different? How would people feel today if Mr. Tominski lived next to them? (CR)
- How did Amen grow and develop in the book? What did Amen first think about Mr. Tominski? How did her views change by the end of the story? (E)

- Describe Mr. Tominski. (F) Illustrate what you think he looks like. (EX)
- What did Amen mean when she said, "As long as there are words, nobody need ever die." (p. 120)? (I)
- Why did Grandma call Mr. Tominski "the dove magician?" (F)
- Did Mr. Tominski remind you of anyone? Did the twins or Amen? (PC)
- What do you think about the book? Did anything bother you? (E) Write a review and talk about how you feel about the story, the characters, and theme. Would you recommend it for others to read? (EX)

The Other Side by Jacqueline Woodson (2001). New York: G. P. Putnam's Sons. Woodson's simple, eloquent story describes the growing friendship between Clover and Annie, and the racial divide signified by a fence between their two houses. E. B. Lewis's soft, realistic watercolor paintings add a gentleness to this lovely story.

> RL: second grade; IL: through fifth grade; 29 pages

Discussion and Extensions:

- Look at the illustrations. What is the setting (the time and place)? (I)
- Why were Annie and Clover told by their mothers not to climb over the fence that separated their homes? (I)
- Why did the girls become friends? (I)
- Why was Sandra unfriendly to Annie? (I) Do you know anyone like Sandra? (PC)
- Could this story happen today? Would Annie and Clover be discouraged from becoming friends? Would their parents encourage the friendship? (CR)
- Write about Annie and Clover when they are twenty years old. How have they changed? Where do they live? Are they still friends? (P) (EX)

Train to Somewhere by Eve Bunting (1996). New York: Clarion Books. This poignant, sensitive picture book describes the orphan train in the late 1800s and Marianne, the orphan who patiently waits for her mother to reclaim her after leaving her at the steps of St. Christopher's orphanage in New York City. As the train pulls away from each western stop, Marianne is left as younger, prettier girls and strong boys are chosen by loving couples or, more frequently, by individuals wanting free labor. Marianne does find the former, and tenderly gives her mother's feather to the elderly woman with whom she will live. This book supports a time in our history where young immigrants often became homeless, and orphans in New York City were transported west for an uncertain life.

> RL: second grade; IL: through eighth grade; 32 pages

Discussion and Extensions:

- Find out all you can about the orphan trains on the Internet. What often was the fate of orphans adopted by families in the west? (R) What social conditions made life difficult for these children? Do they still exist today? (CR)
- Why did no one want to adopt Marianne? (I)
- What year was it? Read about the conversation between the conductor and Miss Randolph (p. 4). (I)
- Why was the feather so important to Marianne? What did she do with it when she reached the town of Somewhere? (F)
- Fourteen orphans began the journey. When the train stops at Porterville, Illinois, Zachary and two other boys leave the group. Then Marvis Perkins and Nora are chosen as well. Eddie Hartz leaves at the next stop. How many orphans remain when the train leaves Porterville? (EX)
- Eddie Hartz is seven years old, and Susan and Nora are five years old. Marianne is older than Eddie. Who is the youngest? Who is the oldest? Make up another problem to solve. (EX)
- What do you think became of Marvis? Do you think Miss Randolph was worried about her? Reread page 12 for clues to support your prediction. (P)
- Write an epilogue that begins two years after Marianne leaves the train in Somewhere. What has her life been like? (P) (EX)

POETRY

Rhyme

Hoop Queens by Charles R. Smith Jr. (2003). Cambridge, Mass.: Candlewick Press. Twelve action-packed poems with image-making, rhyming words describe the individual styles and talents of twelve professional basketball women. The short poems are written in bold white print against colorful backgrounds and full-length action photographs of players that include Lisa Leslie, Sheryl Swoopes, Natalie Williams, and Tina Thompson.

RL: NA; IL: fourth grade and up; 35 pages

Discussion and Extensions:

- Reread a favorite poem several times. Why do you like the poem? What feelings do you have when you read it? How do the words make you think of the player? (E)
- How tall is Margo Dydek? In what countries does Dawn Staley play? (F)
- Select a favorite poem and illustrate how the words make you feel. Choose crayons or paints. Make a collage out of words that describe the player. (EX)
- Read the poet's notes about his research on each player (pp. 32–33) and use the web to find out more about her. (R)
- Why does the poet compare Lisa Leslie to a gazelle? (I)
- Choose your favorite basketball player. Think of a list of action words and adjectives that describe how she or he plays basketball. Use the words to write a poem that describes how the individual looks and moves on the court. Illustrate your poem with photographs or your own illustrations. (EX)
- Charles Smith uses at least fifteen action "ing" words to describe Ticha Penicheiro. Write an acrostic poem about Ticha and use action words with "ing" endings. (DL) (EX)

Joyful Noise: Poems for Two Voices by Paul Fleischman (1988). New York: Harper and Row. Fleischman's poems describe a plethora of

insects, including grasshoppers, mayflies, book lice, and
cicadas. The text, written on both sides of the page, is
written for two readers: when lines are parallel students
read in unison.

RL: NA; IL: all
ages; 44 pages,
14 poems

Discussion and Extensions:

- In pairs, select a poem, rehearse, and then read to classmates
  (Readers' Theater). What did you learn about your insect? (EX)
- After reading an insect poem, write a short, descriptive paragraph
  about it. Refer back to the poem for information about the insect.
  Draw a picture of your insect at the bottom of the page. (EX)
- Do you like the illustrations? What do you think about the pen and
  ink? Would you prefer color? (E)
- What do you think about the book? What is your favorite poem?
  Why? (E)
- Write an acrostic poem using the name of your favorite insect. (EX)

Life Doesn't Frighten Me by Maya Angelou (1978) paintings by Jean-
Michel Basquiat (1993). New York: Stewart, Tabori, and Chang. Stark,
bold paintings support the poet's rhyming verse and
empowering theme of facing life's challenges with
courage and determination. Bad dogs, shadows, big
ghosts, dragons, and tough guys are some of the scary

RL: NA; IL: all
ages; 26 pages

images depicted in the author's repetitive verse and the illustrator's ex-
pressionistic paintings. Rhyming patterns include *al* (wall, hall, all), *ou*
(loud, cloud), *ight* (fight, night) and *ar* (park, dark).

Discussion and Extensions:

- What do you think about the artist's paintings? How do they make
  you feel? Which painting is your favorite? Why? (E)
- Name some of the scary things that the poet describes in her poem.
  (F) What are some things you could add to the list? (PC)
- What advice does Maya Angelou give to readers to face the scary
  things in life? What is her magic charm? (I)
- How does the poem make you feel? Illustrate your feelings, using
  bright paints like the artist Jean-Michel Basquiat. (PC)
- What questions would you like to ask Maya Angelou? (SQ)

- Use some of the author's rhyming words (night, fight; loud, cloud; flame, pane; park, dark) and others that you think of and write and illustrate your own poem about how life doesn't frighten you at all. (EX)

My Many Colored Days by Dr. Seuss (1996). New York: Knopf. One or two rhyming sentences per page, bold type, and colorful, splashy paintings by Steve Johnson and Lou Fancher illustrate color words and the feelings that they evoke. Brown slow days, quiet green days, and sad purple days are a few of the feelings that are beautifully portrayed in this easy to read picture book.

> RL: NA; IL: all ages; 28 pages

Discussion and Extensions:

- Read the color poems. Do you feel the same as the author on purple days, black days, red or orange days? How are your color days the same or different? (PC)
- Select favorite colors (e.g., red, blue, orange) and write a poem or short phrase about how each color makes you feel. Use descriptive words to convey your feelings and illustrate each page. (EX)
- Select two days of the week (e.g., Monday, Friday) and use colors to illustrate how you feel on these days. Write two or three words or phrases that describe your illustrations. (EX)
- Act out the poem. For example, on bright red days, use body movements and facial expressions to convey the author's feeling. (EX)
- How did the picture book make you feel? Did you like it? What did you think about the illustrations? (E)

Oh, the Places You'll Go! by Dr. Seuss (1990). New York: Random House. This picture book has delightful rhyming text, short lines, and themes that are appropriate for older readers. Perseverance, overcoming problems, taking advantage of opportunities, and self-confidence are all part of this uplifting, inspiring book.

> RL: NA; IL: all ages; 43 pages

Discussion and Extensions:

- Have you ever felt "all hung up" and "left in a lurch"? "In a slump" or "lonely"? (PC) What does the author tell you to do? (I)

- What is the "Waiting Place" and why is it so dangerous? (I) Think about a time when you have been there. What does it feel like? How did you escape? (PC) Illustrate your experience. (EX)
- What does the author mean when he says that "Life's a great balancing act" (p. 39)? (I)
- What is the main idea or theme of the picture book? (E)
- How does the book make you feel? What is your favorite part? What do you think about the illustrations? Write a review for other readers. (E)

Rhyme and Free Verse

Extra Innings: Baseball Poems, selected by Lee Bennett Hopkins (1993). New York: Harcourt Brace. This collection describes baseball—the game, the players, the instruction, and much more. Hopkins includes classics such as "Casey at the Bat" (Ernest Thayer) as well as other shorter poems that celebrate the mighty game of baseball. Each poem is accompanied by realistic, splashy watercolor illustrations.

> RL: NA; IL: all ages; 39 pages

Discussion and Extensions:

- Read "Prediction: School P.E." (Isabel Joshlin Glaser) (p.12). What is the poem about? Look at the illustration. How does the artist support the main idea? (I) Describe a time when you have felt like Natalie. (PC)
- Read "The Baseball" (Sandra Liatsos) (p. 19). To what does the poet compare the baseball? Why does she use this comparison? To what other object could you compare a fast ball? (DL)
- Read "The Umpire" (Milton Bracker) (p. 27). Do you agree with the poet? What do you think about umpires? What do you think about the poem? (E)
- Read "Casey at the Bat" (Ernest Lawrence Thayer) (p. 15–16). What did the poet mean when he said that baseball player Cooney died at first base? (I) Read the sixth stanza. What adjectives would you use to describe Casey? (DL) Why did Casey strike out? (I)
- Which poem is your favorite? Why? (E)

My Man Blue by Nikki Grimes (1999). New York: Penguin Putnam. Descriptive vocabulary and magical verse, along with bold, colorful impressionistic paintings by Jerome Lagarrigue, describe the complex, loving relationship between a young asthmatic boy and his mother's friend, Blue.

RL: NA; IL: through ninth grade; 29 pages

Discussion and Extensions:

- What adjectives does the author use to describe Blue? His hands, his smile, his teeth, his clothes? (DL) Draw a picture of Blue. (EX)
- Why does Damon want to be like Blue? (I) Does Blue remind you of anyone you know? (PC)
- At first, Damon is jealous of Blue. Why? Why does Blue want to be Damon's friend? (I)
- What characteristics do Blue and Damon have in common? (I)
- When Damon is afraid to climb a tree, what does Blue tell Damon to do with fear? When Damon is angry that he has to miss a stick-ball game because of asthma, what does Blue tell Damon about anger? (I) What do you think about Blue's advice? Would you follow it? Why or why not? (PC)
- Write about what Damon and Blue are doing in five years. Has anything changed? How do they feel? Write the story from Blue's perspective. (EX)
- How does the poem make you feel? What do you think about the illustrations? (E)

Put Your Eyes Up Here and Other School Poems by Kalli Dakos (2003). New York: Simon and Schuster. Rhyme and free verse poems talk about favorite teachers, not-so-favorite school subjects, and an artistic student who doesn't read very well. Several poems have parts for three to

RL: NA; IL: through sixth grade; 64 pages

seven students and are perfect for Readers' Theater. (See "A Gift for Ms. Roys," pp. 59–60; "Children's Poems about the Snow," p. 44; and "I Don't Believe in Ghosts," pp. 24–28.) G. Brain Karas's illustrations support this humorous, witty collection.

Discussion and Extensions:

- Read "In Color" (p. 17). Ms. Roys wrote a poem about a student who doesn't read very well. What do you think she wrote about? Find clues in the poem. (I)
- Read "Special Eyeball" (p. 20). What are Ms. Roys's special eyeballs? (I)
- Select your favorite poem. Why do you like it? How does it make you feel? (E)
- Read "Don't Go Near It" (p. 55). Draw a picture about what happens to Penny when she talks to the magic wand. (EX)
- Readers' Theater: Read "A Gift for Ms. Roys" (pp. 59–60). Select a favorite part, practice it, and read the poem with six other friends. (EX)
- Read "A Good-bye Note to Ms. Roys." (pp. 62–63). Why does Penny think that Ms. Roys is so special? (I). Does Ms. Roys remind you of a teacher you know? (PC)

Reach for the Moon by Samantha Abeel (1994). Duluth, Minn.: Pfeifer-Hamilton. This collection of image-provoking poems and essays was written by a thirteen-year-old student with learning disabilities. Throughout her poems, Samantha Abeel uses metaphors to lead readers into

RL: NA; IL: seventh grade and up; 39 pages

her creative world. For instance, in "Self Portrait" she compares herself to a tree, its bark, roots, and leaves subtly infusing her learning disability in math to explain in part who she is (p. 4). Bright, colorful watercolors by Charles Murphy accompany her poems.

Discussion and Extensions:

- Read "Self Portrait" (p. 4). Why does the poet compare herself to a tree? What similar characteristics do both have? (I) Think about your strengths. To what object or animal would you compare yourself? (PC)
- Read "Alone" (p. 11). What is the poem about? How does she feel about being alone? (I) How do you feel about being alone? Write a short poem, illustrate a picture, or write a short paragraph about how you feel when you are "alone." (EX)

- Read "If You Want to See" (p. 27). What does the poet say about the past, the present, the future? (I)
- Read "Samantha's Story" (pp 1-3). What is her advice to students who have a disability? (F)
- Following Samantha's advice, list all of your strengths. What do you do with your strengths, or the things that you are good at? (PC)
- What do you think about Samantha's poems? (E)
- What questions would you like to ask Samantha? (SQ)

The Dream Keeper and Other Poems by Langston Hughes (1994). New York: Knopf. This is a beautiful collection of poems organized around six headings (e.g., "The Dream Keeper," "Sea Charm," "Dressed Up"). Many poems are short yet full of meaning and figurative language. Most are free verse, though some rhyme. Favorites include *Sea Calm* and *Poem* (both six-line poems) and *Dreams* (eight lines). The following literature extensions pertain to the well-known poem, *Dreams* (p. 4).

RL: NA; IL: all ages; 80 pages

Discussion and Extensions:

- The poet compares lost dreams to a frozen, snow-covered field. Why did the poet use these words to describe lost dreams? What words would you use? What places remind you of lost dreams? (DL)
- The poet compares dreams that die to a bird with a broken wing. Why do you think he makes this comparison? What words would you use? (DL)
- What does this poem make you think of? What broken dreams or fulfilled dreams do you have? What are your dreams? Write, draw, paint, or act out your dreams. (EX)
- Choose one color or several colors to show how you feel about the poem (EX).
- What questions do you have? What would you like to ask the poet? (SQ)

The World According to Dogs: Poems and Teen Voices by Joyce Sidman (2003). Boston: Houghton Mifflin. Free verse poems, striking black-and-white photographs, and teen essays portray how dogs enter our lives and capture our hearts. Image-making po- ems range from three lines to five stanzas. Through short essays, teens describe their own dogs and the memories that make them so special. This is a beautiful and touching book for dog lovers.

RL: NA; IL: sixth grade and up; 72 pages

Discussion and Extensions:

- Read "Always Take a Dog" (p. 2). What is the poet saying? What can dogs discover that we often miss? (I)
- Read "How to Meet a New Idea Based on the Study of a Dog" (p. 8). What can a dog teach us when we are faced with new information? What does the dog do if the idea is good? Bad? What does the poet suggest that we do? (I)
- Write a short essay about your dog or pet. Describe your dog sleeping, playing, eating, or some memory that is special to you. Take a photograph. (EX)
- Read "Separation" (p. 30). Why does the seal remind the poet of her dog? (I) Describe a time when you were separated from your pet or someone you cared about. What did it feel like? (PC)
- Read "Foot Fetish" (p. 45). Have you ever felt like the poet? What does it feel like to have a dog tickle your feet? (PC)
- Read "This Is a Secret" (p. 49). What is the author's secret? (I)
- Which photograph did you like the best? Why? Which poem did you like the best? Why? How did it make you feel? (E)

Visiting Langston by Willie Perdomo (2002). New York: Henry Holt. Large print, two to four lines per page, with repetitive, familiar vocabulary plus colorful, collage illustrations describe a visit to Langston Hughes's house by a young Harlem poet and her father. Rhythm, rhyme, and jazz ring throughout the text with detailed illustrations that give the reader a glimpse into the famous poet's brown limestone house. In about 160 words, the author creates a musical mood that is highlighted by the glorious, patterned illustrations.

RL: NA; IL: all ages; 27 pages

Discussion and Extensions:

- Look at the collage illustrations. What information tells you about the poet's life? (I)

- Draw a picture of your favorite room or place. Use three or four descriptive words to describe the feelings you have when you are there. (EX)
- Read the poet's notes at the beginning of the picture book. Find out more information about Langston Hughes on the web. (R) Write a bio-poem about Langston Hughes. What did he love? How did he feel? What were his accomplishments? What did he fear? (EX)
- What does the young poet in the story find out about Langston Hughes? (F)
- If Langston Hughes were alive, what questions would you like to ask him? (SQ)
- How does the poem make you feel? What words do you like? What collage illustration is your favorite? (E)
- Make a collage illustration about your life. (EX)

4

RESOURCES

Numerous resources help teachers select and use children's literature and provide literacy experiences that support individual growth and promote self-esteem. Professional books and journals provide research-based instructional strategies, assessment practices, and literature recommendations for teachers who work with struggling readers. Web resources recommend children's books, literacy lessons, computer software, interactive student games, and inquiry-based activities that promote literacy and higher-level thinking skills. The following books, professional journals, and websites are a sampling of resources that support literacy and student voice.

PROFESSIONAL RESOURCES

Books

Ada, A. 2003. *A magical encounter: Latino children's literature in the classroom*. Boston, Mass.: Allyn and Bacon.
   Provides lists and examples of Latino children's books and instructional strategies that promote understanding of text and critical literacy skills.
Ada, A., and F. I. Campoy. 2004. *Authors in the classroom: A transformative education process*. New York: Allyn and Bacon.

Supports teachers, students, parents, and caretakers as authors in writing their own stories and provides examples of books authored by teachers, students, and families.

Brozo, W. 2002. *To be a boy, to be a reader: Engaging teen and preteen boys in active literacy*. Newark, Del.: International Reading Association.

Provides numerous titles and practical ideas for using literature to improve boys' thinking about text and motivation to read.

Gunning, T. 1998. *Best books for beginning readers*. Boston, Mass.: Allyn and Bacon.

Provides information on determining book levels and lists more than 1,000 children's books for beginning readers.

Fehring, H., and P. Green, eds. 2001. *Critical literacy: A collection of articles from the Australian Literacy Educators' Association*. Norwood, South Australia: Australian Literacy Educators' Association.

A collection of articles about critical literacy and the role of the teachers in enabling students to understand the power of language and multiple meanings of texts.

Fountas, I., and G. Pinnell. 1999. *Matching books to readers: Using leveled books in guided reading, K–3*. Portsmouth, N.H.: Heinemann.

Aids teachers in selecting appropriate books for children with a wide range of achievement levels and gives an extensive guided reading book list, appendix 3.

Mantione, R., and S. Smead. 2003. *Weaving through words: Using the arts to teach reading comprehension strategies*. Newark, Del.: International Reading Association.

Provides examples of lessons that integrate reading comprehension and the arts (e.g., mural painting, drama, music, songwriting, fabric collage).

McCormack, R., and J. Paratore, eds. 2003. *After early intervention, then what? Teaching struggling readers in grades 3 and beyond*. Newark, Del.: International Reading Association.

Edited chapters explore effective avenues for literacy development (e.g., Readers' Theater, reading guides, book clubs) in various instructional settings.

McKenna, M. 2002. *Help for struggling readers: Strategies for grades 3–8*. New York: Guilford Press.

Includes suggestions and strategies for decoding, fluency, vocabulary, questioning, and formats for comprehension lessons.

Valmont, W. 2003. *Technology for literacy teaching and learning*. New York: Houghton Mifflin.

Provides information and suggestions for using technology in various aspects of literacy development, such as listening and speaking, writing, word recognition, and critical thinking and reading.

Journals

English Journal. Urbana, Ill. National Council of Teachers of English.
> Provides a forum for teachers (middle school and high school) to share ideas about the teaching of English and language arts; published bimonthly by NCTE.

Exceptional Children. Arlington, Va.: Council for Exceptional Children.
> Publishes original research on the education and development of exceptional infants, children, and youth, and articles on professional issues; published four times a year.

The Horn Book Magazine. Boston, Mass.
> Includes features, book reviews, and columns about children's literature; published six times a year.

The Journal of Adolescent and Adult Literacy. Newark, Del.: International Reading Association.
> Reflects current theory, research, and practice for individuals teaching reading to adolescents and adults; published eight times a year. Lists trade books selected by middle and secondary students in "Young Adult Choices" (November issue).

Learning Disabilities Research and Practice. Boston, Mass.: Division for Learning Disabilities, Council for Exceptional Children.
> Presents current research and information for practitioners in the field of learning disabilities. Also includes book reviews, diagnostic instruments, educational materials, and software; published four times a year.

The Reading Teacher. Newark, Del.: International Reading Association.
> For teachers interested in teaching literacy and intended as a forum for theory, research, and practice in literacy education; published eight times a year. Lists trade books selected by children in "Children's Choices" (October issue) and those selected by teachers in "Teacher's Choices" (November issue).

Teaching Exceptional Children. Arlington, Va.: Council for Exceptional Children.
> For teachers of children with disabilities and those who are gifted, and features articles about practical methods and materials for classroom use; published six times a year.

Organizations

The following professional organizations provide professional development opportunities for their members through national conventions, journals, newsletters, and other services noted on their websites. All support teachers and teacher education.

The Council for Exceptional Children (CEC) (www.cec.sped.org)
   An international professional organization whose goal is to improve educational outcomes for individuals with exceptionalities, students with disabilities, and/or gifted students, and serves as advocates for governmental poli-
   cies, sets standards, and provides continual professional development.
The International Dyslexia Association (IDA) (www.interdys.org)
   The oldest learning disabilities organization in the nation dedicated to helping individuals with dyslexia, their families, and the communities that support them, and serves as a comprehensive forum for parents, educators, and
   researchers to share experiences, methods, and research.
The International Reading Association (IRA) (www.reading.org)
   An international service organization whose mission is to improve reading instruction and promote the lifetime reading habit. The IRA publishes five
   journals, an electronic journal (www.readingonline.org), as well as professional books and a bimonthly newspaper.
The National Council of Teachers of English (NCTE) (www.ncte.org)
   An organization dedicated to improving the teaching and learning of English
   and English language arts at all levels of education (K–12) and provides a forum
   for professionals and opportunities for teachers to continue professional growth.

READING STANDARDS

Standards for the English language arts, copublished by the National
Council of Teachers of English (NCTE) and the International Reading
Association (IRA), include twelve standards that address opportunities
and resources to ensure the development of literacy skills. Of specific
relevance to this text are the following standards:

- Students read a wide range of print and nonprint texts (fiction,
  nonfiction, classic, and contemporary works) to build an understanding of texts, of themselves, and of the cultures of the United
  States and the world;
- Students apply knowledge of language structure and language conventions, media techniques, figurative language and genre to create, critique, and discuss print and nonprint texts;
- Students participate as knowledgeable, reflective, creative, and
  critical members of a variety of literacy communities.

See the International Reading Association website for links to the twelve standards for the English language arts and standards for reading professionals: www.reading.org.

TECHNOLOGICAL RESOURCES

Web Sources for Children's Literature

A to Z Teachers Stuff: http://AtoZTeacherStuff.com
   Provides themes and links to thematic units and lesson plans, book activities, books, and professional resources organized by theme.
Bibliomania: www.bibliomania.com
   Provides links to free online literature (more than 2,000 classic texts), literature book notes, author biographies, study guides to the most-read books, and help for teachers.
Carol Hurst's Children's Literature Site: www.carolhurst.com/index.html
   Provides links to children's books (feature books and more recommended books arranged by title, author, and grade level), subjects in children's books (curriculum areas, theme, and other subjects), and professional resources.
Children's Literature: www.childrenslit.com
   Provides links to features (author and illustrators, teaching materials, reviews by theme), events and related sites (book lists, literacy criticism, reading/literacy organizations, kids, parents, teachers, and librarian resources), awards and prizes, and database services (comprehensive database and instructional materials).
The Children's Literature Web Guide: www.acs.ucalgary.ca/~dkbrown/index.html
   Provides links to authors (A–Z), Readers' Theater, recommended books, films, videos, recordings, and computer software.
The American Library Association: www.ala.org/parents/index.html
   Provides links to books, activities, and video selections such as KidsConnect Favorite Web Sites, Notable Children's Web Sites; Book Awards (Caldecott Medal, Coretta Scott King Award, Newberry Medal, Pura Belpri Award); Notable Children's Computer Software; Children's Recordings; and Children's Videos.
Reading Rainbow: http://gpn.unl.edu/rainbow
   Provides links to classroom resources (alphabetical listing of book titles, videos, teacher guides, related websites for teachers), Reading Rainbow

booklist (by title, author, illustrator), national broadcast schedule, and information about Reading Rainbow (research, awards, press releases).

The International Reading Association: www.reading.org
Provides links to choice book lists that include Teacher's Choices, Children's Choices, and Young Adult Choices (resources listed in the *Reading Teacher* and *Journal of Adolescent and Adult Literacy*, respectively).

Scholastic Book Club: http://teacher.scholastic.com/
Provides links to book clubs, software club, and the teacher resource center that includes ready-to-go lessons.

TeenReads: www.teenreads.com
Provides links to author reviews, identifies books, and provides short author biographies. Author profiles include Walter Dean Myers, Jacqueline Woodson, and Jack Gantos. Recipients of the Michael L. Printz Award (literary excellence for young adult literature) are listed.

Websites for Interactive Literacy Activities

Cyberteens: www.cyberteens.com
Cyberteens is an online community for young adults worldwide to share thoughts and ideas, and provides creative avenues for reading, writing (e.g., poetry, nonfiction), and art.

Dave's ESL Café: http://eslcafe.com
Provides link to Forum for Teachers that supports literacy (e.g., story boxes, wordless picture book) and links for students that support literature and family activities. This is a good resource for English as a Second Language (ESL) students.

Disney: www.disney.com
Provides links such as FamilyFun with activities, crafts and recipes, and the Technology and Innovations Center, which takes readers on a journey to explore and learn about the brain.

Funbrain: www.funbrain.com
Provides links to Kids and Games, Parents, and Teachers that provide interactive activities for children. For example, link to Teacher, then Curriculum Guide, then Game Subject Areas and find fifteen games from which to choose. Paint by Idiom helps children identify the idiom meaning by selecting one of four correct statements. Wacky Tales requires students to select adjectives, adverbs, nouns, etc. that are then combined to form a "wacky story."

Kid's Corner: http://kids.ot.com
Provides links to Puzzles, Hangman, Your Turn, and Web Surfin'. Hangman requires students to select a letter from a selection of choices to spell a word.

Like the familiar game, the more wrong choices, the more the hangman's noose is filled-in. Your Turn publishes children's poetry and stories. Guidelines for submission follow the children's literary or artistic work.

LeapFrog: www.leapfrog.com

LeapFrog toys and games is an interactive learning system that provides toys and games for children of all ages (infant, toddler, preschool; grade school, middle school to high school—Quantum Pad and cartridges). For example, the Quantum Pad player, for children in third to fifth grades, holds books (with corresponding cartridge) that provide interactive activities and games relating to the story in the player.

PBS: http://PBSKids.com

Provides numerous educational links that include Zoom where kids can send in reviews to favorite books (also movies, TV, and music) such as *Because of Winn-Dixie* and *The Giver*.

WebQuests: http://edweb.sdsu.edu/WebQuest/WebQuest.html

WebQuest is an inquiry-oriented activity that requires students to find, analyze, and synthesize information on the web. This site, hosted by the Educational Technology Department at San Diego State University (Bernie Dodge), provides WebQuests listed at grade level (K–2; 3–5; 6–8; 9–12; adult) and by subject (e.g., English/language arts, art and music). For example, a Web-Quest described on this site about the Aztecs provides the task, the process (includes a game plan with clues and resources), and conclusion (how to create a report to share information).

Lesson Plans on the Web

AskERIC: http://ericir.syr.edu/Virtual/Lessons

This good source includes more than 2,000 exemplary lesson plans written by teachers. Lesson plans are categorized by subject such as arts, computer science, language arts, mathematics, and social studies. The AskERIC Lesson Plan Collection is grouped according to Pre-K, kindergarten throughout twelfth grade. Lesson plans include description of the lesson, goals, objectives, materials, procedures, and assessment. Readers can contact the writer (teacher) by e-mail or address. AskEric also encourages teachers to share exemplary lesson plans and provides information regarding submission and selection criteria.

Gem: http://geminfo.org

The Gateway to Educational Materials (GEM) is a consortium effort that provides access to collections of Internet-based educational material that are available on various federal, state, university, nonprofit, and commercial Internet sites.

ReadWriteThink: www.readwritethink.org

An informative website that offers links to standards-based lesson plans, IRA/NCTE Standards for the English Language Arts, and peer-reviewed web resources that include over one hundred links that are rated on a three-star system (three stars indicate an exemplary site, two stars a recommended site, and one star a promising site).

Software that Supports Literacy

Inspiration: webmaster@inspiration.com

Inspiration software helps learners brainstorm, organize, plan, and create ideas through visual diagrams (mapping). Inspiration 7 (grades six–adult) and Kidspiration (K–5) help students organize information, understand concepts, and express thoughts through software that supports visual thinking and learning.

Earobics Step 1 and Step 2: www.earobics.com

Cognitive Concepts Earobics teaches phonological awareness, auditory processing, and phonics skills. Earobics Step 1 (ages four to seven) teaches phonological awareness, auditory processing, and introductory phonics skills through six interactive games and over 300 levels of play. Earobics Step 2 (ages seven to ten), addresses skills in Step 1 but at more advanced levels through five interactive games with roughly 600 levels of play. The software addresses individual needs through adjusting the game play to the skill level and progress of the student.

Edmark Reading Program: www.proedinc.com

The Edmark Reading Program uses a whole-word approach to teach recognition and comprehension of words for students with developmental or learning disabilities and ESL students. The program teaches sight word recognition and comprehension and uses the word in a story context. Students hear and read original illustrated stories on the computer, building upon words mastered in previous lessons.

Lexia Learning Systems: www.lexialearning.com

The Lexia programs provide a structured phonics approach based on Orton-Gillingham principles that help students develop phonological awareness, sound-symbol correspondence, fluency, and vocabulary. This program includes assessment software (Lexia Quick Reading Test, ages five-adult; Lexia Comprehension Reading Test, K-adult) and skills development programs (ages four to six; five to eight; nine to adult). For example, Lexia Phonics Based Reading (ages five to eight) includes short and long vowel words, blends, diagraphs, two-syllable words, and close comprehension. Reading

S.O.S. (Strategies for Older Students) (ages nine to adult) reinforces prior word attack skills and provides practice decoding multisyllabic words.

Start to Finish Books: www.donjohnston.com

This high-interest, low-vocabulary series is geared to students with reading difficulties in fourth grade through high school. The Gold series (grades four through twelve) has a 2.0–3.0 reading level; the Blue series (grades seven through twelve) has a 4.0–5.0 reading level. Books are rewritten to eliminate difficult language and include a computer book (CD-ROM) with words that are highlighted as they are narrated, a corresponding paperback book, and audiocassette. Start to Finish topics include history, famous people, adventure, sports, original mysteries, and retellings of classic literature.

Websites Directed to Special Needs

The Children with Disabilities Website: http://www.childrenwithdisabilities.ncjrs.org

Provides information about advocacy, education, employment, recreation, technical assistance, and transportation covering a broad array of developmental, physical, and emotional disabilities. The site includes links to federal, state, and national resources, grants and funding, and research and statistics.

Council for Exceptional Children: www.cec.sped.org

Provides links that introduce readers to the council, professional development and training opportunities, membership, publications, CEC discussion forums, and international programs.

The International Dyslexia Association: www.interdys.org

Provides links to educators, children, college students, parents, and adults with information about dyslexia and support systems relevant for each group.

LDOnline: www.ldonline.org

Provides links that include LDOnline (resource for children and parents and teachers of children with learning disabilities), LDOnline.org (readers' e-mail questions and concerns), Learning Disabilities OnLine: KidZone (publishes children's work), and Reading Rockets (provides research findings and suggestions for parents, teachers, tutors, and child care providers).

National Center for Learning Disabilities (NCLD): www.LD.org

Provides links to the NCLD mission, news and insights about LD, special sections for teen and adults, research, local and national programs and services, and early literacy screening.

Parent Advocacy Coalition for Educational Rights Center (PACER): www.pacer.org

Provides links to mission, publications, national sites, and legislation.

Author Websites or E-mail Addresses

Avi: www.avi-writer.com/
Judy Blume: www.judyblume.com
Betsy Byars: www.betsybyars.com
Andrew Clements: www.frindle.com
Christopher Paul Curtis: kids@randomhouse.com
Katherine Patterson: www.terabithia.com/
Gary Paulsen: www.randomhouse.com/features/garypaulsen
Patricia Polacco: www.patriciapolacco.com/
Jon Scieszka and Lane Smith: www.chucklebait.com/
Lemony Snicket: www.lemonysnicket.com/
Jerry Spinelli: www.carr.lib.md.us/authco/spinelli-j.htm

Books on Audiotape

Books on audiotape provide reinforcement and models for fluent reading. Struggling readers have an opportunity to follow along in the text, discover unfamiliar words, and hear fluent, expressive reading that supports comprehension. The following audio selections are books that have been described in chapter 3. Books that precede or follow selected books are also included since the characters, theme, and often the same problem are extended and will interest readers who have enjoyed a previous book by the same author (e.g., *Brian's Winter, Brian's Return*, Gary Paulsen; *Joey Pigza Swallowed the Key*, Jack Gantos).

The Bad Beginning: A Series of Unfortunate Event, Lemony Snicket, Listening Library, Random House
Because of Winn-Dixie, Kate DiCamillo, Listening Library, Random House
Brian's Return, Gary Paulsen, Listening Library, Random House
Brian's Winter, Gary Paulsen, Listening Library, Random House
Double Fudge, Judy Blume, Listening Library, Random House
Frindle, Andrew Clements, Listening Library, Random House
Gathering Blue, Lois Lowry, Listening Library, Random House
Handbook for Boys, Walter Dean Myers, HarperCollins Audio
Hatchet, Gary Paulsen, Listening Library, Random House
Holes, Louis Sachar, Listening Library, Random House
The Janitor's Boy, Andrew Clements, Listening Library, Random House
Joey Pigza Loses Control, Jack Gantos, Listening Library, Random House

Joey Pigza Swallowed the Key, Jack Gantos, Listening Library, Random House
Locomotion, Jacqueline Woodson, Recorded Books
The Miserable Mills: A Series of Unfortunate Events, Lemony Snicket, Harper-
   Collins Audio
Monster, Walter Dean Myers, Listening Library, Random House
Pictures of Hollis Wood, Patricia Reilly Giff, Listening Library
The Reptile Room: A Series of Unfortunate Events, Lemony Snicket, Listening
   Library, Random House
Sarah Plain and Tall, Patricia MacLahlan, Harper Collins Audio
What Would Joey Do? Jack Gantos, Listening Library, Random House

PARENT RESOURCES

Parents and caretakers frequently have questions and concerns about their
child's reading performance, books to select, or procedures to follow. Often there is not enough time during parent conferences or school staffings
to allow for the open exchange of dialogue between parents or caretakers
and school professionals. The following resources include books and
newsletters written for parents and caretakers and those interested in family literacy.

Anderson, W., S. Chitwood, and D. Hayden. 1997. *Negotiating the special ed-
ucation maze: A guide for parents and teachers*. 3rd ed. Bethesda, Md.: Wood-
bine House.
   Written by parent advocates (who are also parents), this informative book an-
   swers questions regarding a variety of issues surrounding the special education process, such as the referral process and placements, the Individualized
   Education Program (IEP), and due process.
Cullinan, B. 1992. *Read to me: Raising kids who love to read*. New York:
Scholastic.
   The author provides reading tips, literature selections, and developmental
   aspects that pertain to reading and reading interests that address preschool-
   ers through eleven- and twelve-year-olds.
DeBruin-Parecki, A., and B. Krol-Sinclair, eds. 2003. *Family literacy: From
theory to practice*. Newark, Del.: International Reading Association.
   This collection supports the field of family literacy, connects theory to practice,
   and explores various facets of family literacy that include diverse family literacy programs and school- and community-supported family literacy programs.

Leonhardt, M. 1995. *Parents who love reading, kids who don't: How it happens and what you can do about it*. New York: Three Rivers Press.

> The author, who is both a parent and teacher, writes about how parents can promote a love of reading for reluctant, disinterested, and/or struggling readers and provides a list of reading selections for middle school and high school readers.

Lilly, E., and C. Green. 2004. *Developing partnerships with families through children's literature*. Upper Saddle River, N.J.: Pearson Education, Merrill Prentice Hall.

> This informative and readable book addresses family involvement and children's literature, and focuses on infants through five-year-olds. Chapters include information relevant for all age ranges, such as principles for working with culturally diverse families, different types of families (e.g., single parent, multiracial, immigrant and migrant families) and transitions (death, adoption, divorce).

Perspectives is a newsletter of the Internal Dyslexia Association that includes the column "Parent to Parent," written especially for parents of children who have learning disabilities such as dyslexia.

Reading Today is a bimonthly newspaper of International Reading Association (IRA) and includes a Department for Parents and Reading that provides professional tips and reading resources for parents.

Schwab Learning (www.schwablearning.org) is an online guide developed by the Charles Helen Schwab Foundation especially for parents of children identified with learning disabilities, and provides parent materials, such as "A Parents' Guide to Differences and Disabilities in Learning."

Williams, N. 2002. *Selecting and using good books for struggling readers: A resource for parents and caregivers*. Lanham, Maryland: Scarecrow Education.

> This resource helps parents and caretakers locate and use quality children's literature that is appropriate for struggling readers. It provides recommended books and reading levels, and categorizes selections by interest.

CHILDREN'S BOOK TITLES BY INTEREST

NONFICTION

Athletes/Sports

Hoops with Swoopes, Susan Kuklin with Sheryl Swoopes (2001). New York: Jump at the Sun, Hyperion Books for Children.

Jackie Robinson, Kenneth Rudeen (1974). New York: Harper Trophy, Harper-Collins.

Lou Gehrig: The Luckiest Man, David Adler (1997). New York: Gulliver Books, Harcourt Brace.

Roberto Clemente, James Buckley Jr. (2002). London: Dorling Kindersley.

Sammy Sosa: Home Run Hero, Jeff Savage (2000). Minneapolis, Minn.: Lerner Publications.

Shooting for the Moon: The Amazing Life and Times of Annie Oakley, Stephen Krensky (2001). New York: Melanie Kroupa Books, Farrar Straus and Giroux.

Fine Arts: Dance, Music, Art

Dance, Bill T. Jones, Susan Kuklin (1998). New York: Hyperion Books for Children.

Duke Ellington, Andrea Davis Pinkney (1998). New York: Hyperion Books for Children.

Frida, Jonah Winter (2002). New York: Arthur A. Levine Books, an imprint of Scholastic Press.

Hokusai: The Man Who Painted a Mountain, Deborah Kogan Ray (2001). New York: Frances Foster Books, Farrar, Straus and Giroux.

Magic Windows, Carman Lomas Garza (1999). San Francisco, Calif.: Children's Book Press.

Thank You, Mr. Falker, Patricia Polacco (1998). New York: Putnam and Grosset.

When Marian Sang, Pam Muñoz Ryan (2002). New York: Scholastic Press.

Leaders of Social Justice

Champion: The Story of Muhammad Ali, Jim Haskins (2002). New York: Walter.

Free at Last! The Story of Martin Luther King, Jr., Angela Bull (2001). London: Dorling Kindersley Readers.

The Greatest: Muhammad Ali, Walter Dean Myers (2001). New York: Scholastic, Inc.

Malcolm X: A Fire Burning Brightly, Walter Dean Myers (2000). New York: HarperCollins.

Martin's Big Words, Doreen Rappaport (2001). New York: Hyperion Books for Children.

Writers

Authors by Request: An Inside Look at Your Favorite Writers, Janie Campbell and Cathy Collison (2002). Hillsboro, Ore.: Beyond Words Publishing.

Bad Boy: A Memoir, Walter Dean Myers (2001). New York: HarperCollins. (Teacher Resource).

Calling the Doves, Juan Felipe Herrera (1995). San Francisco, Calif.: Children's Book Press.

Coming Home: From the Life of Langston Hughes, Floyd Cooper (1994). New York: Putman and Grosset.

My Life in Dog Years, Gary Paulsen (1998). New York: Random House.

FICTION

Fantasy: Animals

Ereth's Birthday, Avi (2000). New York: HarperTrophy.

The Grand Escape, Phyllis Reynolds Naylor (1993). Bantam Doubleday Dell.

The Good Dog, Avi (2001). New York: Aladdin Paperbacks.
Gooseberry Park, Cynthia Rylant (1995). New York: Scholastic.
Poppy, Avi (1995). New York: Avon Books.
Tales from the House of Bunnicula: Howie Monroe and the Doghouse of Doom, James Howe (2002). New York: Atheneum Books for Young Readers.

Fantasy: Ghosts

The Doll in the Garden, Mary Downing Hahn (1989). New York: Avon Books.
The Heavenly Village, Cynthia Rylant (1999). New York: Scholastic, Inc.
Pleasing the Ghost, Sharon Creech (1996). New York: HarperTrophy.
Something Upstairs, Avi (1988). New York: Avon Books.

Fairy Tales

Just Ella, Margaret Peterson Haddix (1999). New York: Simon and Schuster.
The Frog Prince Continued, Jon Scieszka (1991). New York: Viking.
The Three Little Wolves and the Big Bad Pig, Eugene Trivizas (1993). New York: Macmillan.
The Three Pigs, David Wiesner (2001). New York: Clarion Books, Houghton Mifflin.
The True Story of the 3 Little Pigs, Jon Scieszka (1989). New York: Viking.

Identity/ Solving Problems

REM World, Rodman Philbrick (2000). New York: Scholastic Signature, Scholastic.
Maniac Magee, Jerry Spinelli (1990). New York: Little Brown.
Stargirl, Jerry Spinelli (2000). New York: Knopf.
Things Not Seen, Andrew Clements (2002). New York: Philomel Books, Penguin Putnam.

Mystery

Gathering Blue, Lois Lowry (2000). New York: Random House.
Holes, Louis Sachar (1998). New York: Frances Foster Books, Farrar, Straus and Giroux.
The Hostile Hospital: A Series of Unfortunate Events, Lemony Snicket (2001). New York: HarperCollins.

The Miserable Mill: A Series of Unfortunate Events, Lemony Snicket (2000). New York: HarperCollins.
The Reptile Room: A Series of Unfortunate Events, Lemony Snicket (1999). New York: HarperCollins.

Time Travel/Outer Space

Company's Coming, Arthur Yorinks (1988). Hyperion Books for Children.
Company's Going, Arthur Yorinks (2001). Hyperion Books for Children.
Hey Kid, Want to Buy a Bridge? The Time Warp Trio, Jon Scieszka (2002). New York: Puffin Books, the Penguin Group.
Running Out of Time, Margaret Peterson Haddix (1997). New York: Aladdin Paperbacks, Simon and Schuster.
Sam Samurai, The Time Warp Trio, Jon Scieszka (2001). New York: Puffin Books, the Penguin Group.

CONTEMPORARY REALISTIC FICTION

Adventure/Survival

Brian's Winter, Gary Paulsen (1996). Bantam Doubleday Dell Books for Young Readers, a division of Bantam Doubleday Dell.
Gleam and Glow, Eve Bunting (2001). New York: Harcourt.
Hatchet, Gary Paulsen (1987). New York: Bradbury Press, Macmillan.

Friendship/Romance

The Friends, Kazumi Yumoto (1992) (1998 USA translation). New York: Bantam Doubleday Dell Books for Young Readers.
Pacific Crossing, Gary Soto (1992). Fla.: Harcourt.
Seventh Grade, from *Baseball in April and Other Stories*, Gary Soto (1990). New York: Harcourt.

Humor

The Boy Who Lost His Face, Louis Sachar (1989). New York: Del Yearling, a division of Random House.
Cockroach Cooties, Lawrence Yep (2000). New York: Hyperion Books for Children.

Double Fudge, Judy Blume (2002). New York: Dutton Children's Books, Penguin Putnam Books for Young Readers.

Hoot, Carl Hiaasen (2002) (Newbery Honor). New York: Knopf.

Frindle, Andrew Clements (1996). New York: Aladdin Paperbacks, Simon and Schuster.

Jackson Jones and the Puddle of Thorns, Mary Quattlebaum (1994). New York: Delacorte Press.

Identity/Solving Problems

Because of Winn-Dixie, Kate DiCamillo (2000). Cambridge, Mass.: Candlewick Press.

A Blue-Eyed Daisy, Cynthia Rylant (1985, Rylant; 2001, Aladdin). New York: Aladdin Paperbacks, an imprint of Simon & Schuster.

Egg-Drop Blues, Jacqueline Turner Banks (1995). Boston, Mass.: Houghton Mifflin.

Handbook for Boys, Walter Dean Myers (2002). New York: HarperCollins.

It Doesn't Have to Be This Way, Luis J. Rodriguez (1999). San Francisco, Calif.: Children's Book Press.

The Jacket, Andrew Clements (2002). New York: Aladdin Books, an imprint of Simon and Schuster.

The Janitor's Boy, Andrew Clements (2000). New York: Aladdin Books, an imprint of Simon and Schuster.

Joey Pigza Loses Control, Jack Gantos (2000). New York: Farrar, Straus and Giroux.

Joey Pigza Swallowed the Key, Jack Gantos (1998). New York: HarperCollins.

just Juice, Karen Hesse (1998). New York: Scholastic.

Locomotion, Jacqueline Woodson (2003). New York: G. P. Putnam's Sons.

Miracle's Boys, Jacqueline Woodson (2000). New York: G. P. Putnam's Sons.

Monster, Walter Dean Myers (1999). New York: HarperCollins.

Pictures of Hollis Woods, Patricia Reilly Giff (2002). Wendy Lamb Books, imprint of Random House.

Searching for David's Heart, Cherie Bennett (1998). New York: Scholastic.

The Skin I'm In, Sharon Flake (1998). New York: Jump at the Sun, Hyperion Paperbacks for Children.

Vanishing, Bruce Brookes (1999). New York: A Laura Geringer Book, HarperCollins.

What Would Joey Do? Jack Gantos (2002). New York: Farrar, Straus and Giroux.

Mystery

Dead Letter, A Herculeah Jones Mystery, Betsy Byars (1996). New York: Puffin Books, Penguin Group.

Death's Door, A Herculeah Jones Mystery, Betsy Byars (1997). New York: Puffin Books, Penguin Group.

Disappearing Acts, A Herculeah Jones Mystery, Betsy Byars (1998). New York: Puffin Books, Penguin Group.

No More Magic, Avi (1975). New York: Random House.

HISTORICAL REALISTIC FICTION

Adventure/Survival

Crispin, Avi (2002). New York: Hyperion Books.

The Fighting Ground, Avi (1984). New York: HarperCollins Children's Books.

Freedom's Wings: Corey's Diary, Kentucky to Ohio, Sharon Dennis Wyeth (2001). New York: Scholastic.

The Girl Who Chased Away Sorrow: The Diary of Sarah Nita, a Navajo Girl, Ann Turner (1999). New York: Scholastic.

The Journal of Jessie Smoke: A Cherokee Boy, Joseph Bruchac (2001). New York: Scholastic.

The Journal of Wong Ming-Chung: A Chinese Miner, Lawrence Yep (2000). New York: Scholastic.

One Candle, Eve Bunting (2002). New York: HarperCollins.

Friendship/Romance

Pink and Say, Patricia Polacco (1994). Philomel Books, a division of the Putnam and Grosset Group.

Sarah, Plain and Tall, Patricia MacLachlan (1985). New York: HarpherTrophy.

Identity/Solving Problems

Keeper of the Doves, Betsy Byars (2002). New York: Viking.

The Other Side, Jacqueline Woodson (2001). New York: Penguin Putnam Books.

Train to Somewhere, Eve Bunting (1996). New York: Clarion Books.

POETRY

Rhyme

Hoop Queens, Charles R. Smith, Jr. (2003). Cambridge, Mass.: Candlewick Press.

Joyful Noise: Poems for Two Voices, Paul Fleischman (1988). New York: Harper and Row.

Life Doesn't Frighten Me, Maya Angelou (1978, 1993). New York: Stewart, Tabori, and Chang

My Many Colored Days, Dr. Seuss (1996). New York: Knopf.

Oh, the Places You'll Go! Dr. Seuss (1960). New York: Random House.

Rhyme and Free Verse

The Dream Keeper, Langston Hughes (1994). New York: Knopf.

Extra Endings: Baseball Poems, Lee Bennett Hopkins (1993). New York: Harcourt Brace.

My Man Blue, Nikki Grimes (1999). New York: Dial Books for Young Readers, Penguin Putnam.

Put Your Eyes Up Here and Other School Poems, Kalli Dakos (2003). New York: Simon and Schuster.

Reach for the Moon, Samantha Abeel (1994). Duluth, Minn.: Pfeifer-Hamilton.

Visiting Langston, Willie Perdomo (2002). New York: Henry Holt.

The World According to Dogs: Poems and Teen Voices, Joyce Sidman (2003). Boston: Houghton Mifflin.

B

CHILDREN'S BOOK TITLES BY GENRE

PICTURE BOOKS

Calling the Doves, Juan Felipe Herrera (1995). San Francisco, Calif.: Children's Book Press.

Champion: The Story of Muhammad Ali, Jim Haskins (2002). New York: Walter.

Coming Home: From the Life of Langston Hughes, Floyd Cooper (1994). New York: Putnam and Grosset Group.

Company's Coming, Arthur Yorinks (1988). Hyperion Books for Children.

Company's Going, Arthur Yorinks (2001). Hyperion Books for Children.

Dance, Bill T. Jones, Susan Kuklin (1998). New York: Hyperion Books for Children.

Duke Ellington, Andrea Davis Pinkney (1998). New York: Hyperion Books for Children.

Frida, Jonah Winter (2002). New York: Arthur A. Levin Books, an imprint of Scholastic Press.

The Frog Prince Continued, Jon Scieszka (1991). New York: Viking.

Gleam and Glow, Eve Bunting (2001). New York: Harcourt, Inc.

The Greatest: Muhammad Ali, Walter Dean Myers (2001). New York: Scholastic, Inc.

Hokusai: The Man Who Painted a Mountain (2001). New York: Frances Foster Books, Farrar, Straus and Giroux.

Hoops with Swoopes, Susan Kuklin with Sheryl Swoopes (2001). New York: Jump at the Sun, Hyperion Books for Children.

It Doesn't Have to Be This Way, Luis J. Rodriguez (1999). San Francisco, Calif.: Children's Book Press.

Lou Gehrig: The Luckiest Man, David Adler (1997). New York: Gulliver Books, Harcourt Brace.

Magic Windows, Carman Lomas Garza (1999). San Francisco, Calif.: Children's Book Press.

Malcolm X: A Fire Burning Brightly, Walter Dean Myers (2001). New York: HarperCollins.

Martin's Big Words, Doreen Rappaport (2001). New York: Hyperion Books for Children.

One Candle, Eve Bunting (2002). New York: HarperCollins.

The Other Side, Jacqueline Woodson (2001). New York: Penguin Putnam Books.

Pink and Say, Patricia Polacco (1994). Philomel Books, a division of Putnam and Grosset Group.

Shooting for the Moon: The Amazing Life and Times of Annie Oakley, Stephen Krensky (2001). New York: Melanie Kroupa Books, Farrar Straus and Giroux.

Thank You, Mr. Falker, Patricia Polacco (1998). New York Putnam and Grosset Group.

The Three Little Wolves and the Big Bad Pig, Eugene Trivizas (1993). New York: Macmillan.

The Three Pigs, David Wiesner (2001). New York: Clarion Books, Houghton Mifflin.

Train to Somewhere, Eve Bunting (1996). New York: Clarion Books.

The True Story of the 3 Little Pigs, Jon Scieszka (1989). New York: Viking.

When Marian Sang, Pam Muñoz Ryan (2002). New York: Scholastic Press.

SHORT CHAPTER BOOKS AND SHORT NOVELS (UP TO 140 PAGES)

Authors by Request: An Inside Look at Your Favorite Writers, Janie Campbell and Cathy Collison (2002). Hillsboro, Oregon: Beyond Words Publishing Co.

A Blue-Eyed Daisy, Cynthia Rylant (1985, Rylant; 2001, Aladdin). New York: Aladdin Paperbacks, an imprint of Simon and Schuster.

Brian's Winter, Gary Paulsen (1996). Bantam Doubleday Del Books for Young Readers, a division of Bantam Doubleday Dell Publishing Group.

Cockroach Cooties, Lawrence Yep (2000). New York: Hyperion Books for Children.

Death's Door, A Herculeah Jones Mystery, Betsy Byars (1996). New York: Puffin Books, Penguin Group.

Disappearing Acts, A Herculeah Jones Mystery, Betsy Byars (1998). New York: Puffin Books, Penguin Group.

The Doll in the Garden, Mary Downing Hahn (1989). New York: Avon Books.

Egg-Drop Blues, Jacqueline Turner Banks (1995). Boston, Mass.: Houghton Mifflin.

Freedom's Wings: Corey's Diary, Kentucky to Ohio, Sharon Dennis Wyeth (2001). New York: Scholastic.

Frindle, Andrew Clements (1996). New York: Aladdin Paperback, Simon and Schuster.

Gooseberry Park, Cynthia Rylant (1995). New York: Scholastic.

The Grand Escape, Phyllis Reynolds Naylor (1993). New York: Bantam Doubleday Dell.

The Heavenly Village, Cynthia Rylant (1999). New York: Scholastic.

Hey Kid, Want to Buy a Bridge? The Time Warp Trio, Jon Scieszka (2002). New York: Puffin Books, the Penguin Group.

The Jacket, Andrew Clements (2002). New York: Aladdin Books, an imprint of Simon and Schuster.

Jackson Jones and the Puddle of Thorns, Mary Quattlebaum (1994). New York: Delacorte Press.

The Janitor's Son, Andrew Clements (2000). New York: Aladdin Books, an imprint of Simon and Schuster.

Just Juice, Karen Hesse (1998). New York: Scholastic.

Keeper of the Doves, Betsy Byars (2002). New York: Viking.

Locomotion, Jacqueline Woodson (2003). New York: G.P. Putnam's Sons.

Miracle's Boys, Jacqueline Woodson (2000). New York: G.P. Putnam's Sons.

No More Magic, Avi (1975). New York: Random House.

Pacific Crossing, Gary Soto (1992). Fla.: Harcourt, Inc.

Pleasing the Ghost, Sharon Creech (1996). New York: HarperTrophy.

Sam Samurai, Jon Scieszka (2001). New York: Puffin Books, the Penguin Group.

Sarah, Plain and Tall, Patricia MacLachlan (1985). New York: HarperTrophy.

Seventh Grade, from *Baseball in April and Other Stories*, Gary Soto (1990). New York: Harcourt.

Something Upstairs, Avi (1988). New York: Avon Books.

Tales from the House of Bunnicula: Howie Monroe and the Doghouse of Doom, James Howe (2002). New York: Atheneum Books for Young Readers.

Vanishing, Bruce Brookes (1999). New York: A Laura Geringer Book, HarperCollins

NONFICTION (UP TO 140 PAGES)

Free at Last! The Story of Martin Luther King, Jr., Angela Bull (2001). London: Dorling Kindersley Readers.

Jackie Robinson, Kenneth Rudeen (1974). New York: Harper Trophy, Harper-Collins.

My Life in Dog Years, Gary Paulsen (1998). New York: Random House.

Roberto Clemente, James Buckley Jr. (2002). London: Dorling Kindersley.

Sammy Sosa: Home Run Hero, Jeff Savage (2000). Minneapolis, Minn.: Lerner Publications.

LONGER WORKS OF FICTION

Because of Winn-Dixie, Kate DiCamillo (2000). Cambridge, Mass.: Candlewick Press.

The Boy Who Lost His Face, Louis Sachar (1989). New York: Del Yearling, a division of Random House.

Crispin, Avi (2002). New York: Hyperion Books.

Dead Letter, A Herculeah Jones Mystery. Betsy Byars (1996). New York: Puffin Books, Penguin Group.

Double Fudge, Judy Blume (2002). New York: Dutton Children's Books, Penguin Putnam Books for Young Readers.

Ereth's Birthday, Avi (2001). New York: Harper Trophy.

The Fighting Ground, Avi (1984). New York: HarperCollins Children's Books.

The Friends, Kazumi Yumoto (1992). (1998 USA translation). New York Bantam Doubleday Dell Books for Young Readers.

Gathering Blue, Lois Lowry (2000). New York: Random House.

The Girl Who Chased Away Sorrow: The Diary of Sarah Nita, A Navajo Girl, Ann Turner (1999). New York: Scholastic.

The Good Dog, Avi (2001). New York: Aladdin Paperbacks.

Handbook for Boys, Walter Dean Myers (2002). New York: HarperCollins.

Hatchet, Gary Paulsen (1987). New York: Bradbury Press, Macmillan.

Holes, Louis Sachar (1998). N: Frances Foster Books, Farrar, Straus and Giroux.

Hoot, Carl Hiaasen (2002). New York: Knopf.

The Hostile Hospital: A Series of Unfortunate Events, Lemony Snicket (2000). New York: HarperCollins.

Joey Pigza Loses Control, Jack Gantos (2000). New York: Farrar, Straus and Giroux.

Joey Pigza Swallowed the Key, Jack Gantos (1998). New York: HarperCollins.

The Journal of Jessie Smoke: A Cherokee Boy, Joseph Bruchac (2001). New York: Scholastic.

The Journal of Wong Ming-Chung: A Chinese Miner, Lawrence Yep (2001). New York: Scholastic.

Just Ella, Margaret Peterson Haddix (1999). New York: Simon and Schuster.

Maniac Magee, Jerry Spinelli (1990). New York: Little Brown and Company.

The Miserable Mill: A Series of Unfortunate Events. Lemony Snicket (2000). New York: HarperCollins.

Monster, Walter Dean Myers (1999). New York: HarperCollins.

Pictures of Hollis Woods, Patricia Reilly Giff (2002). Wendy Lamb Books, imprint of Random House.

Poppy, Avi (1995). New York: Avon Books.

REM World, Rodman Philbrick (2000). New York: Scholastic Signature, Scholastic.

The Reptile Room: A Series of Unfortunate Events. Lemony Snicket. (1999). New York: HarperCollins.

Running Out of Time, Margaret Peterson Haddix (1997). New York: Aladdin Paperbacks, Simon and Schuster.

Searching for David's Heart, Cherie Bennett (1998). New York: Scholastic.

The Skin I'm In, Sharon Flake (1998). New York: Jump at the Sun, Hyperion Paperbacks for Children.

Stargirl, Jerry Spinelli (2000). New York: Knopf.

Things Not Seen, Andrew Clements (2002). New York: Philomel Books, Penguin Press.

What Would Joey Do? Jack Gantos (2002). New York: Farrar, Straus and Giroux.

LONGER WORKS OF NONFICTION

Bad Boy: A Memoir, Walter Dean Myers (2001). New York: HarperCollins.

POETRY

The Dream Keeper, Langston Hughes (1994). New York: Knopf.

Extra Endings: Baseball Poems, Lee Bennett Hopkins (1993). New York: Harcourt Brace.

Hoop Queens, Charles R. Smith Jr., Cambridge, Mass.: Candlewick Press.

Joyful Noise: Poems for Two Voices, Paul Fleischman (1988). New York: Harper and Row.

Life Doesn't Frighten Me, Maya Angelou (1978, 1993). New York: Stewart, Tabori, and Chang

My Man Blue, Nikki Grimes (1999). New York: Dial Books for Young Readers, Penguin Putnam, Inc.

My Many Colored Days, Dr. Seuss (1996). New York: Alfred Knopf, Inc.

Oh, the Places You'll Go! Dr. Seuss (1996). New York: Random House.

Put Your Eyes Up Here And Other School Poems, Kali Dakos (2003). New York: Simon and Schuster.

Reach for the Moon, Samantha Abeel (1994). Duluth, Minn.: Pfeifer-Hamilton.

Visiting Langston, Willie Perdomo (2002). New York: Henry Holt.

The World According to Dog: Poems and Teen Voices, Joyce Sidman (2003). Boston: Houghton Mifflin.

C

IDIOMS AND FAMILIAR EXPRESSIONS IN LITERATURE SELECTIONS

The Boy Who Lost His Face, Louis Sachar (1989)
Grew like Pinocchio's nose (p. 98)

Cockroach Cooties, Laurence Yep (2000)
Look at the world through rose-colored glasses (p. 33)

Dead Letter: A Herculeah Jones Mystery, Betsy Byars (1996)
Someone walking on my grave (p. 63)

Double Fudge, Judy Blume (2000)
Let the cat out of the bag (p. 20)
Squeezed like sardines in a can (p. 49)

Egg-Drop Blues, Jacqueline Turner Banks (1995)
Put your money where your mouth is (p. 112)
To thine own self be true (p. 55)
Would a rose by any other name smell as sweet (p. 78)
World beats a path to our door (p. 42)
Wear your heart on your sleeve (p. 43)
Cut off your nose to spite your face (p. 50)

Gooseberry Park, Cynthia Rylant (1995)
Can feel it in my bones (p. 83)

Hoot, Carl Hiaasen (2002)
Wasn't the sharpest knife in the drawer (p. 24)
I'm going out on a limb (p. 219)
Jerking our chain (p. 219)

The Hostile Hospital: A Series of Unfortunate Events, Lemony Snicket
(2001)
A slave to fashion (p. 115)
Butterflies in stomach (172)

The Janitor's Boy, Andrew Clements (2000)
Was a walking fashion ad (p. 16)

The Journal of Wong-Chung: A Chinese Miner, Laurence Yep (2000)
You can tell the quality of a person by the company he keeps (p. 149)

Miracle's Boys, Jacqueline Woodson (2000)
Got a monkey on their back (p. 81)

The Miserable Mill: A Series of Unfortunate Events, Lemony Snicket
(2000)
Let's not split hairs (p. 156)
Quiet as mice (p. 81)
Gum up the works (p. 170)

My World According to Dog: Poems and Teen Voices, Joyce Sidman
(2003)
Dog days; dog-eared; dog-eat-dog; doggy bag; dog's life;
Dog-tired; go to the dogs; in the dog house; let sleeping dogs lie;
Teach an old dog new tricks; work like a dog (p. 71)

No More Magic, Avi (1975)
Put your foot in your mouth (p. 20)
A real zero (p. 43)

Oh, the Places You'll Go! Dr. Seuss (1960)
All hung up (p. 17)
Left in a lurch (p. 17)

Pacific Crossing, Gary Soto (1992)
Blow this place (p. 65)
Hang out (p. 48)
Could eat a horse (p. 84)
Felt a lump in his throat (p. 73)
Born yesterday (p. 73)

Running Out of Time, Margaret Peterson Haddix (1997)
Bite off more than you can chew (p. 142)

The Reptile Room: A Series of Unfortunate Events, Lemony Snicket (1999)
Feeling like a fifth wheel (p. 113)

Sam Samurai, Jon Scieszka (2001)
Now we are toast (p. 46)
Hit him like a lightning bolt (p. 51)
Freaked out (p. 18)
Light bulb went off over my head (p. 28)

Stargirl, J. Spinelli (2000)
I jumped in with both feet (p. 43)
Like deer's eyes caught in headlights (p. 5)
Don't count your chickens before they hatch (p. 147)

Things Not Seen, Andrew Clements (2002)
Get your foot in the door (p. 54)

True Story of the 3 Little Pigs, Jon Scieszka (1991)
Dead as a doornail (p. 19)

INDEX

ABOUT THE AUTHOR

Nancy S. Williams is a professor in the School of Education at DePaul University, Chicago, Illinois. She teaches courses in reading and children's literature, and supervises remediation practica in reading and learning disabilities. She received her Ph.D. from Northwestern University in the field of learning disabilities, her M.A. from Southern Methodist University as a reading specialist, and a B.A.E. from the University of Kansas in art education.

Dr. Williams has been an art instructor, reading specialist, and learning disabilities resource room teacher in public elementary and secondary schools, and has worked as a learning specialist and cognitive rehabilitation therapist in a hospital setting. She served as program coordinator in a collaborative university-school partnership program preparing career-change individuals as teachers and served two years as associate dean in the School of Education.

Dr. Williams has published articles about university-school partnerships as well as literacy, coauthored a book about developing literacy skills through trade books in clinical and classroom settings, and authored a resource book for teachers and another one for parents about how to select and use quality children's literature for students with reading difficulties.